LONDON
RAILWAY STATIONS

Waterloo Station Junction COPY1409/219

LONDON
RAILWAY STATIONS

CHRIS HEATHER

 The National Archives

ROBERT HALE

First published in 2018 by
Robert Hale, an imprint of
The Crowood Press Ltd,
Ramsbury, Marlborough,
Wiltshire SN8 2HR

www.crowood.com

British Library Cataloguing-in-Publication Data
A catalogue record for this book is available from the British Library.

ISBN 978 0 7198 2763 1

Disclaimer
Every reasonable effort has been made to trace and credit illustration
copyright holders. If you own the copyright to an image appearing in this
book and have not been credited, please contact the publisher, who will
be pleased to add a credit in any future edition.

Typeset by Servis Filmsetting Ltd, Stockport, Cheshire
Printed and bound in India by Parksons Graphics

Contents

WHEN THE RAILWAYS BEGAN TO BE built in Britain over 180 years ago, London was already the largest city in the world. With a population of around two million people in 1830, London was not only a capital city: it was the hub of the British Empire, soon to become the largest empire the world had ever seen. No wonder, then, that London became a magnet for business, trade, work and entrepreneurs. A key aspect to this development was the coming of the railway, a transport system that changed the face of London forever.

Nearly three billion rail journeys are undertaken each year in the UK, and nine of the ten busiest stations are in London. Waterloo Station alone deals with a quarter of a million passengers each day. There are thirteen mainline termini in London, more than in any other capital city. Moscow, for example, has only nine mainline stations, while the French capital, Paris, a city of similar age and status to London, has a mere seven. There are two main reasons why London has so many stations: firstly, Britain was the first country to develop a railway system at a time of huge industrialization, when goods and people needed to move around the country, and businessmen saw opportunities to make large profits. London was therefore ahead of the game.

Secondly, the British Government saw no need to provide an overall plan for the railway network across the country, or in the capital. It was left to individual companies to propose new railway lines, seek parliamentary approval, and raise enough capital to get started. This led to huge competition and rivalry between the various railway companies, each one striving to make money by choosing a different 'market', whether it was holiday traffic to Devon, the movement of beer from Burton-on-Trent, daily commuters to London, or collecting goods arriving at the Thames docks. This freedom was fertile ground for engineers and architects to come up with unique buildings and structures, many of which can still be seen today.

The laissez-faire approach to transport infrastructure also led to the duplication of lines, the unnecessary embellishment of buildings, the demolition of housing, vast over-expenditure by companies, and many other issues, which can be seen as good or bad depending on one's perspective. Nevertheless, this is how the railways evolved, and how they came to influence the layout of the capital city we know today.

The story of London's stations is one of co-operation and competition, personal ambition and corporate determination. It includes instances of innovative design, technological invention, devotion to service, and triumph over bureaucracy and difficult physical terrain. All thirteen mainline stations were built during a sixty-four-year period, starting with London Bridge Station, which opened in 1836, and ending with Marylebone, which was the last to open in 1899. Each one has its own personality and its own charms and idiosyncrasies. These were determined by location, the functions the stations were designed to perform, the status of the architect, the pride of the railway company, and of course the amount of money available at the time.

These buildings were new inventions in themselves. No one had created a large railway terminus in a capital city before, and nobody knew how they should look or what they should include, and although mistakes were sometimes made, architects had a free rein to create buildings that would be both functional and impressive. Often they would borrow from the grand styles of classical Greek, Roman and Gothic architecture, and this theme would be extended to the associated railway hotel, many of which are today some of the most richly decorated and luxurious hotels in London. As well as hotels, each station could have a retinue of support buildings: offices, stables, goods yards, signal boxes, bridges, viaducts and railway lines, which provided succour to new urban development along their routes, with housing and businesses contributing to the suburbia that would eventually become Greater London.

This book tells the story of each of these stations, how they came to be positioned where they are, who designed them, and what happened to them over time. Through these pages we meet some of the people who built them, worked in them, passed through them as travellers, and even died in them. A wide variety of human activity can be seen here, each anecdote contributing to the narrative of these vital structures that are so familiar to us, and yet which come from another age – an age of steam, smoke, gas lamps and horses. This was an age when a rented brass foot warmer was the height of luxury, and when hailing a cab from the station meant travelling by two wheels and four hooves.

These stations have survived many changes over the years, some more sympathetic than others, but most of them include preserved examples of their original design, bearing testament to the perception, skill, enthusiasm and foresightedness of their Victorian creators. I would encourage you to visit them, to take in the atmosphere and to spot some of the original features, since all can be reached in a couple of hours quite easily from the Circle Line on the Underground. And I hope this book will bring new light to what may be for you very familiar buildings, and help you to see London's mainline stations through new eyes.

Chris Heather, 2018 ✦

Chapter 1

LONDON BRIDGE, 1836

THE STORY OF LONDON BRIDGE STATION begins with Lieutenant-Colonel George Thomas Landmann, your archetypal Victorian adventurer. A man with an entrepreneurial spirit, he played his part in literally building parts of the British Empire. The son of a German professor, he was born in the grounds of the Royal Military Academy, Woolwich, in 1780. He lived a full and varied life, and his colourful escapades, and his inventiveness and ability to get things done, helped to change the face of London.

Landmann was educated at the Royal Military Academy from the age of fourteen, and went on to join the Royal Engineers two years later in 1795. He was posted to Canada, where he built fortifications and a canal. It is said that he once came across a native Indian tribe who were about to torture and burn a woman and her child from another tribe. Landmann stepped in and bought them for six bottles of rum, and returned them to their own people, receiving valuable animal skins by way of acknowledgement. He later moved on to build bridges in Portugal, and in Spain he commanded troops, and built fortifications as part of the defence of Cadiz. The King of Spain thanked him personally for helping to quell an uprising, and he served in several battles and sieges before returning to England because of ill health in 1812.

He continued to serve in the military in Ireland before retiring from the Army in Yorkshire in 1824. Once retired he embarked on a career in civil engineering, becoming a member of the Institution of Civil Engineers, and was appointed engineer to the Preston and Wyre Railway and Harbour Company, helping to build docks at Fleetwood in Lancashire. It was while working on railway projects that he had the idea of building a railway to the City of London.

In October 1831 Landmann and his colleague George Walter, who had previously tried and failed to launch a railway company called The Southampton and London Railway Dock Company, decided to form a new railway company called the London and Greenwich Railway (L&GR). The line would be a short one of just under four miles, running from Greenwich up towards the City, terminating just to the south-east of London Bridge. London Bridge itself was fairly new at this time, having been completed in 1831, and built by civil engineer John Rennie. This was the bridge that was dismantled and replaced in 1971, having been bought by Robert P. McCulloch, an American oil tycoon, who rebuilt the structure at Lake Havasu in Arizona, USA. It is often said that McCulloch thought he was buying London's iconic Tower Bridge, but this is just an urban myth.

A Viaduct for the L&GR

A shareholder's prospectus for the L&GR was printed in May 1833, listing the company directors, auditors and bankers, with George Landmann proudly highlighted as 'Engineer to the Company'. In it the company acknowledge that constructing a rapid means of conveyance into a central part of 'this great Metropolis presents difficulties of no ordinary magnitude', due to the prospect of interfering with the traffic. To solve this problem they announce that 'This Railway is therefore to be constructed on Arches, and in such a manner that Passengers and Carriages may pass along the Streets which the Line will cross, without being obstructed'. Construction of the track was indeed difficult because of the number of streets already built along the line of the proposed track. Landmann could have created a line with numerous level crossings, but this would have meant slower trains and continual obstruction to road traffic, so an elevated viaduct, high above the streets, was the innovative answer.

This new line would be in direct competition with boat traffic on the Thames, the number of boat passengers up and down the Thames during 1831 being estimated at 400,000. The number of people travelling between Greenwich and the city was about 2,000 per day, and then there were horsedrawn coaches as well, so the L&GR needed to provide fast and reliable transport in order to compete. The L&GR would be a raised railway line supported by a series of 878 brick arches, which Landmann hoped to rent out as stables, shops, workshops and even dwellings. A couple of two-storey show homes were built inside two of the arches, each with six rooms, and two windows on the first floor and a window and door at ground level. However, these arches were not watertight, and the continual noise of the trains made them unsuitable as homes. Nevertheless, the archways did prove popular with light engineering companies and for use as lock-up garages. One arch halfway along the viaduct was converted into a pub, known as the Halfway House Tavern, later the Railway Tavern; it survived from the 1850s until 1967.

To provide for large users of the arches, small connecting transverse doorways were built into the walls of each arch, and these could either be left open or bricked up as required. The problems with damp were eventually solved by the application of a further layer of concrete and asphalt, and early on there were even plans to provide the arches with heating and lighting, although this never came to pass.

The land over which the viaduct was built was quite soft and peaty, and the 400 navvies used to build the structure were forced to dig foundation pits up to twenty-four feet deep, so as to provide enough stability to support the viaduct. Landmann was also obliged to use concrete reinforced foundations, and iron ties to stop the piers spreading and collapsing. It took five years to build the viaduct using sixty million bricks, all made in Sittingbourne, Kent, and transported to the site by barge along the Thames. The cost of the structure was £733,000 (almost double the original estimate of £400,000), much of which was spent on buying the necessary land and property.

Parapet walls were built along the sides of the viaduct, 1.3 metres high to prevent walkers, and any trains that might derail, from leaving the viaduct. The train carriages were specially designed to have a low centre of gravity to give them additional stability along the viaduct. This

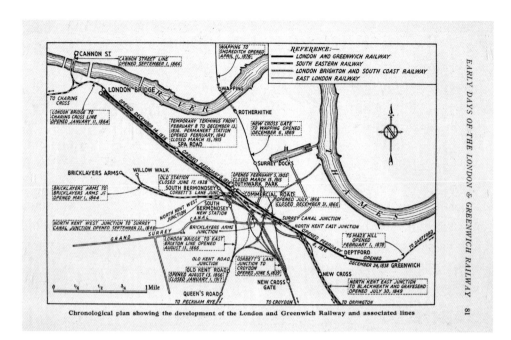

Chronological plan showing the development of the London and Greenwich Railway and associated lines

was the work of George Walter, secretary of the L&GR and founder of the *Railway Magazine*, who turned the usual carriage frame upside down so that the axles were above it rather than underneath it. The heavy frame, now running only four inches above the rails, meant that the vehicles were less likely to sway and rock along the track. The passenger compartments were then raised on blocks up to their previous level, some twenty-five inches above the rails, and this design proved to be very successful in providing stability and avoiding derailments.

Next to the track, along the top of the viaduct, was a 'pedestrian boulevard' along which members of the public could walk at the cost of a penny a time, allowing them to enjoy views across London and the nearby countryside, and to experience the railway close at hand. This walkway was soon converted to an additional train line when the profitability of further train lines was realized. The track itself

was laid initially on to concrete sleepers, but these proved to be too rigid on top of the solid viaduct, and caused problems through noise, vibration and broken wheel axles, so they were eventually replaced by wooden sleepers on a bed of gravel ballast, which provided a little more flexibility.

Another feature of the original plans for the Greenwich Railway was a roadway and gravel path, planted with trees, which was to extend twenty-four feet on each side of the viaduct from end to end. This road was designed to provide access to the archways along the viaduct, and to become a great thoroughfare in itself, along which families and respectable people could promenade in the shade of trees, protected by railway company policemen, and all for the modest cost of 1d per visit. Parts of the road were constructed, but it was not well maintained and soon became rough tracks of muddy ruts and puddles in wet weather. Revenue was collected for a few years (£500 in 1839) but the widening of the viaduct on both sides meant that the avenue was no longer viable, and the tolls were discontinued around 1845.

The whole project provided an early template for many later railway viaducts constructed across London and other cities. Technically speaking the structure is actually nineteen separate viaducts, which are linked together by twenty-seven road bridges. Even today it is the longest run of arches in Britain, and one of the oldest railway viaducts in the world. The original viaduct was widened in places in the 1840s and 1850s along both its north and south sides.

On 9 June 1835 the engine *Royal William*, weighing fourteen tons, carrying several passengers and her tender primed with water and coal, completed a trial run of one mile in four minutes near Blue Anchor Road, watched by company directors and shareholders. A glass of water filled to the brim was placed on one of the stone sleepers, and not a drop was spilled as the engine passed along. More trials took place with full-length trains this time; then on 12 November a carriage came off the tracks, and although it ran a number of yards, no one was injured. Landmann, ever the optimist, congratulated the shareholders on the derailment as it showed how safe the viaduct was even when accidents occurred. *Royal William* was Engine No. 1 of the L&GR, built by Tayleur and Co. at the Vulcan Foundry, and was the first steam engine ever to provide a passenger service in London.

The Sceptics

Not everyone was in favour of the new railway, most notably George Shillibeer, the famous pioneer horse bus proprietor, who had set up a business running twenty omnibuses linking London, Greenwich and Woolwich in 1834. He promoted the idea that train travel was dangerous, and by contrast his buses would neither blow up nor explode 'like mines', that no one need fear travelling in them. He said that the railroad was not worth investing in as it would be put out of business by horse buses. Unfortunately for him he was proved wrong when his buses were all seized by the Stamp Office when he fell into arrears with his payments shortly after the new railway opened.

Similar scepticism was evident in the comments of the *Quarterly Review* publication for March 1835, when speeds of eighteen miles per hour were expected of the new railway: 'We should as soon expect the people of Woolwich to be fired off from one of Congreve's rockets as trust themselves to such a machine going at such a rate.'

The Opening of the L&GR

The first section of the London and Greenwich Railway line opened to the public on 8 February 1836, running from Deptford to Spar Road, near the junction with Rouel Road, and such was the excitement generated by the new service that it managed to carry 13,000 passengers on its first day alone. This effectively makes Spar Road Station London's first ever railway terminus, although it was little more than a couple of wooden platforms atop the viaduct, and a rickety wooden staircase up from ground level. The line soon reached London Bridge Station, which opened on 14 December 1836, after several postponements. Formal invitation cards for the opening ceremony had been printed for Tuesday 1 November, but the event was put off and the cards were over-printed with 14 December.

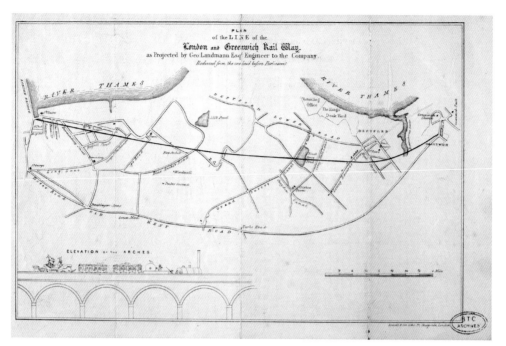

The London
and Greenwich
Railway and
associated
lines. RAIL1075/146

The opening ceremony was a grand occasion, where four trains made their way down to Deptford at a steady twenty miles per hour, carrying the Right Honourable Thomas Kelly, Lord Mayor, and various city dignitaries in the first train, while the band of the Scots Guards played them off. A short distance outside the station the Mayor's train halted while the three other trains passed by on the other line in procession. Then the three trains stopped while the Mayor's train passed by to applause, leading the way to Deptford, where the band of the Coldstream Guards welcomed them playing both 'popular and national music'.

Whilst at Deptford the Lord Mayor inspected the company works underneath the station, before walking from the High Street to the Ravensbourne River where he inspected the bridge. He then received a deputation from the inhabitants of Deptford, gave a speech, and then returned to London by train, this time reaching speeds of up to thirty miles per hour. Around 2,000 people attended the ceremony, with 500 enjoying a formal dinner afterwards, where they celebrated the railways reaching the capital.

London's First Passenger Railway Terminus

London Bridge Station can therefore be said to be London's first passenger railway terminus, beating the London and Birmingham Railway's Euston Station, which opened on 20 July 1837. The actual station building, however, was very basic. On the south side of the London end of the viaduct was a simple three-storey building which housed the booking office and the company offices. The rest of the station simply comprised two platforms serving three railway tracks. There were no waiting rooms and no roof or train shed of any kind. Passengers would climb steps, or use a ramp to make it up to platform level, where

amidst the firing of cannon, the ringing of church bells, and the cheers of an excited crowd.

Spa Road, the only intermediate station, which was filled to excess with the multitude there assembled, was reached with almost the swiftness of a discharged Congreve rocket, and afterwards Deptford, where a vast concourse, in carriages and on foot, awaited the visitors, with a second band of music, which then took the place of the first on the return journey.

being specially illuminated, and a grand pyrotechnic display concluded the programme of the opening celebration. The shows and the illuminations were, however, continued into the New Year, and in order that the railway might be further attractively exhibited as " a work of art," and made to " draw," a band of musicians " played in " the passengers at both the London and Deptford ends until the traffic was fairly established ! The railway was completed through to Greenwich towards

DWELLING-HOUSES IN THE ARCHES UNDER THE GREENWICH RAILWAY.

The trains ran at intervals of half an hour during the day, and among the various shows at either end we read that " a special attraction " was provided at the Deptford terminus in the model of a submarine destroyer, called a naval torpedo, the invention of the Earl of Dundonald. At night coloured rows of lamps were displayed along the whole length of the railway on either side, the stations

the end of the following year, being opened with a further imposing ceremony on December 24, 1838, when we are told that " the Managing Director of the railway " (4 miles in length, be it observed) was attended in his movements with a degree of pomp and splendour calculated to excite the admiration of beholders ! " The Greenwich terminus was built in what at that time was looked upon as " a scale of

they would wait in all weathers for their train to depart.

First Customer, the L&CR

The L&GR did not set out to make a statement with their station, as other railway companies would try to do in the coming years. Instead their plan was to stake a claim to a convenient access point to London, and then make their fortune by charging other railway companies

for access to it. From the outset the directors planned for the potential continuation of the line from Greenwich down into Kent and Sussex, and even to Dover for connection with the continent by boat. By keeping the station simple they could save on initial outlay, yet at the same time they owned enough land around the terminus to expand at a later date once they had become fully established. Their first customer was the London and Croydon Railway Company (L&CR), which used the L&GR line to build their own terminus to the north of the L&GR station, opening on 5 June 1839.

Further back along the line the L&CR built their own viaduct to take their trains south, branching out from the original arches at a junction near Corbett's Lane, and forming the world's first railway junction. At the point where the tracks diverged a 'policeman', or signalman, was positioned in a wooden tower so as to control trains moving between the two lines. At night time signalling in the form of red and white lights was introduced, and the tower therefore became known as the Corbett's Lane Lighthouse. This was in effect the world's first signal box.

Water Refuelling System

Engines leaving London Bridge Station would always run 'backwards', with their tender or bunker first. This was because there was no water crane at London Bridge, and water was taken on board at the other end of the line at Greenwich, where, on arrival, the carriages would be uncoupled and the engine would continue beyond the station a little way on to a turntable, next to which the water crane was located. The turntable was basically a short section of track that could revolve, lining up with a number of different lines, above a shallow circular pit. Once refuelled with water the turntable would rotate and direct the engine on to the appropriate line for the return journey to London. The system worked well, apart from on one occasion in 1861 when a driver backed his engine on to the turntable, not realizing that the track was still aligned with the tracks for London. His tender ended up in the pit, thus blocking the only water source for the whole of the line.

New Lines for the SER and the L&BR

The South Eastern Railway and the London and Brighton Railway also began to run over the London and Croydon tracks and into London Bridge Station, joining the original London and Greenwich tracks at Corbett's Lane, Deptford. Due to the increase in traffic the viaduct was widened between 1840 and 1842 to four lines from Corbett's Lane to London Bridge. The new lines were added along the south side of the viaduct, although they were intended for use by the Croydon, Brighton and SER trains, whose station was on the northern side of the L&GR station. This would have required a complicated points system, and the danger of trains crossing each other's tracks, so the directors of all the companies concerned agreed to swap stations – the L&GR would move into the new L&CR station, while the remaining companies would take the original station, which they promptly decided to demolish in order to build a bigger one.

A New Joint Station

By 1844 a new, much larger, Italian palazzo-style joint station had been built, designed by Lewis Cubitt and Henry Roberts, and large enough to cope with the additional traffic from the SER and the L&BR. Early drawings of the proposed station show it as having an ornate bell tower at one end, although in actual fact the tower was never built and the station was never finished.

When the service began the company provided carriages for three classes of passenger. First class compartments had horse-hair cushions and sloping seats with leather inserts, while second class coaches had narrow, upright seats. Accommodation for third class passengers was very basic, being open wagons without seats, known as 'standipedes' or 'stanups'. Complaints regarding such poor accommodation were brushed aside by the directors, who considered there was 'no justification for the murmur. If the people would insist on travelling at so cheap a rate, it was only reasonable that they should pay the penalty in a certain amount of discomfort!' The third class option had been withdrawn by 1842 when the secretary of the L&GR, a Mr Akerman, replied to a government survey regarding third class passengers – his letter provides a useful insight to the accommodation provided on their trains:

The trains on this line run every quarter of an hour each way. There are no third class, but only first and second class passengers. The carriages on this Railway are similar to those of the Blackwall, the second class passengers occupying the end division and the first class the middle. The end divisions hold about 20 second class passengers

and are 7 feet wide by 5 feet long and 7 feet from the floor to the roof. They are without seats.

The two first class divisions are 7 feet wide by 5 feet long, and hold eight passengers. All the above carriages are provided with undersprings, draw-springs and buffing apparatus, and are mounted on six wheels.

The L&GR were charging the other railway companies high fees for the use of their facilities, 3d per passenger, and so the SER obtained permission to build their own terminus at Bricklayers Arms, also opening in 1844. This meant that only the L&GR and L&BR were left using London Bridge Station. In 1845 the L&GR relented and reduced their fees to 1¼d per passenger, and leased the whole of the line to the SER for a term of 999 years. The SER now controlled the approach to London Bridge Station.

Early sketch of the advertisement 'Trains to London Bridge every fifteen minutes'. ZSPC11/345

London Bridge Station Divided

In 1846 the L&CR merged with the L&BR and others to form the London, Brighton and South Coast Railway (LBSCR), which used the joint station until 1849 when it was knocked down in order to build a larger station. Meanwhile the SER took over the L&GR station on the northern side of the site, which they rebuilt between 1847 and 1850 to a design by Samuel Beazley, incorporating a solid wall between the two stations, emphasizing the division of the station into two separate halves. Their Bricklayers Arms station was then converted into a goods depot, then a parcel depot in 1969, and in 1981 the line was closed.

The LBSCR build the Terminus Hotel in 1861, alongside the station. It was leased to a private hotel company, but was not very popular, being on the south side of the river, and in 1892 it was taken back by the railway company and turned into office accommodation. It was built on land previously owned by St Thomas's Hospital, and occupied by low grade housing. The architect of the hotel was Henry Currey, one-time colleague of William Cubitt and designer of St Thomas's Hospital. The building was constructed from white bricks with Portland stone dressings. There were 250 rooms, and the hotel cost £111,000 to build. Sadly, the building was badly damaged by bombing in 1941 and was demolished thereafter.

Provision of Services

London Bridge Station continued to evolve in a divided way, as two separate stations, run by different companies, each with their own style and agenda, the SER controlling the northern side, and the newly formed London, Brighton and South Coast Railway managing the southern half. This meant that rules and procedures in place on one side of the station would not apply in the other half. For example, in 1888 the SER entered into an agreement with the London Road Car Company for them to provide a horse-drawn omnibus service to pick up and deliver passengers to the station. This gave the car company permission to traverse the SER-owned approaches to the station, but not those owned by the LBSCR, for which they would pay the SER three shillings per week for each omnibus used. By 1913 the service had been replaced or supplemented by a Mr Frederick Tindle, who used his single horse-drawn omnibus to provide a similar service, paying the SER five shillings per week for the privilege. However, his omnibus was specifically forbidden to loiter on the approach, and his servants were not permitted to tout for business.

Some services did end up the same in both halves of the station, although this was more by luck than through planning. Mr John Perrett was already running the refreshment rooms in the SER side of the station when in November 1862 he answered an advertisement in *The Times* newspaper for someone to run the refreshment room in the LBSCR side. He wrote three letters to the company explaining that he was ideally situated to provide the service, and was willing to pay £1,000 per year in rental, or 5 per cent more than anyone else submitting a tender. The LBSCR, perhaps realizing that Mr Perrett was perfectly positioned to provide the service, but also that he was so keen to strike a deal that he could be persuaded to pay a little more, offered him a contract at £1,400 per year for the following seven years. Mr Perrett accepted the offer on 3 December, and passengers could therefore enjoy the same standard of tea and cake in whichever half of the station they found themselves.

Increasing Traffic Brings Problems

Passenger numbers grew rapidly in the next few years, and both halves of the station undertook changes to deal with increased traffic. The SER side converted into a through station, with new tracks out to Charing Cross, while the LBSCR side grew in terms of additional, longer platforms. The viaduct into the station was widened to carry eleven tracks, and the LBSCR introduced electric motive power via an overhead cable system for some services. This was replaced between 1926 and 1928 by the third rail system of electric power, overseen by the new Southern Railway Company formed by the amalgamation of the railways companies of southern England in 1923. So finally, after eighty-four years, the two halves of London Bridge Station were united and run as a single entity.

London Bridge Station had begun to get a reputation for being difficult to navigate – confusing for passengers and for being overcrowded. The decisions of the various rival railway companies in the mid-1800s had badly affected the design of the station, leaving lasting repercussions for passengers, making it one of the most difficult London stations to navigate. However, in 1928 a footbridge was installed joining the two halves of the station for the first time, and allowing passengers to make connections without having to leave one half of the station to walk round to the other half. This was a great improvement considering the station dealt with around a quarter of a million passengers each day. However, an article in the *Railway Magazine* published in February 1937 shows that the problems were still present:

> Perhaps as a result of its promiscuous begetting, London Bridge station has not the most efficient layout in the world. This is noticeable particularly during the evening rush hour when in the Central section passengers stream in from a dozen different entrances, and if their destinations should take them over to platforms 16–22 they may become entangled with a succession of newspaper vehicles, post office vans, parcel

Hop pickers leaving at midnight from London Bridge, 1891. ZPER34/99

vans and packages, and also with a cross-flow of passengers speeding towards the low-level and Eastern sections, who meet another cross-flow coming in the opposite directions over the footbridges and through the narrow single barrier between the Central section and the low-level section.

During the 1930s there was an average of 446 people employed at the station. This included two assistant station masters, sixteen booking clerks, thirty-seven ticket collectors, seventy-two parcel porters, sixty-seven platform porters, seventy-four passenger guards, and a host of other workers. The station also ran a post office, which turned over £75,000 per year, much of its business coming from the sale of 107,000 postal orders, the sending of 52,000 telegrams, and the issuing of 196 dog licences and 854 radio licences – all services no longer required or available at post offices today.

London Bridge Station in World War II

During World War II some of the roads and archways under the station were used as air-raid shelters. One particular shelter was located along Stainer Street, running inside a London Bridge Station arch between Tooley Street and St Thomas Street. In October 1940 the shelter was examined by Home Office engineers and health inspectors, and the conditions they discovered were so shocking that one inspector stated that he found it difficult to put his impressions into words. The premises regularly held around 3,000 people sheltering each night, yet there was only one tap for drinking water, there was no flooring apart from trodden earth, and the few toilets that were present were entirely inadequate and located behind temporary screens with sacking material hanging as 'doors'.

There were four exits from the shelter, one of which was large enough to allow trucks access, and next to this was a room where the hides of freshly killed horses were piled. Blood and the accompanying refuse was seen flowing out into the passage where the shelter bedding was stored. The medical officer reported that this was the finest breeding ground for an epidemic that he had ever seen.

There was a first-aid post, but it was manned by volunteers who had no medical training, and most of the medical supplies had gone missing anyway. Many of the passageways through the shelter were blocked by filthy bedding, and passengers using the railway during an air raid often preferred to take the risk of being above ground rather than staying down in the shelter. Even so, many people did use the shelter, and marshals were present to try to supervise the crowds – but anything they said was usually ignored. The police had refused to oversee the shelter since it was on railway property and they believed that railway staff should be running it. The Home Office report on the shelter ends with the inspector's assurance that he had never seen anything more entirely sickening than these public shelters. He states that 120 more toilets should be installed, the rubbish should be cleared from the passageways, and three-tiered bunk beds supplied, along with at least one paid first-aider.

The Commissioner of the Metropolitan Police, Sir Philip Game, in a letter to the Home Office sent on 28 October 1940, made his thoughts clear on these shelters, calling them 'death traps'. His concern was that the shelters were not strong enough to protect those inside. The crown of the arch was not proof against even a small fifty kilo bomb, and the long passageway needed to be divided up by 'baffle walls', which would contain any explosion damage to one small section of the tunnel. He urged the government to seek the advice of someone who had knowledge not only of the strength of materials, but also the blast and destructive effect of heavy bombs.

Sure enough, on the night of 17 February 1941, a 500 kilogram bomb hit the Strainer Street shelter, and another landed just outside in St Thomas's Street. The second bomb was a delayed action device, falling at 10.30pm, but not exploding until the following morning. Out of the 300 people sheltering, sixty-eight were killed and 175 injured. Many of those killed were hit by the steel doors, each weighing ten tonnes and installed at the entrance to the shelter, and designed to protect those inside, which were blown down into the shelter when the bomb hit, crushing those underneath. Other casualties were medical staff from nearby Guys Hospital, who were tending to the injured when the second bomb exploded. The depth of the bomb crater and the amount of rubble were so great that it is thought that the bodies of some victims were never recovered, and still lie beneath the road that passes through the tunnel today.

Modernization

After the war, electrification continued under British Railways from 1948, but by the 1960s, in common with other London termini, the dated layout, combined with sheer passenger numbers, meant that the station needed modernizing. Between 1972 and 1978 the station underwent major improvement works, receiving new signalling, a new concourse, and a new roof over the old SER platforms, although the original arched roof over the Brighton side was repaired and preserved. During the 1980s and 1990s the station remained largely unchanged, the main development being that platforms were extended to enable the use of twelve-carriage trains.

Below ground, however, the work on extending the Jubilee Line to East London

Bomb damage at London Bridge Station, 1940–41. RAIL648/132

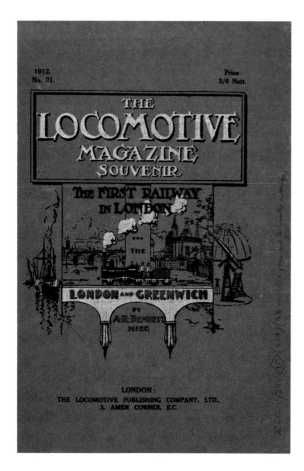

'The First Railway in London.' ZSPC11-345

provided the stimulus to redevelop the station's link to the Underground system during the 1990s, converting the rundown area under the station platforms into a bright new booking hall, with shops and cafés added to the new complex, which opened in 1999.

The Building of the Shard

Perhaps the biggest change to the appearance of London Bridge Station came between 2009 and 2012 with the building of a ninety-five-storey glass-clad skyscraper, stretching 309 metres into the air and towering above the station: the Shard, and Britain's tallest building. It was built as part of the London Bridge Quarter redevelopment, which in effect provided a new roof over the terminal level concourse of the station.

Before it was built Italian architect Renzo Piano said he had designed it to look like a futuristic church spire emerging from the Thames, reminiscent of church steeples seen in old paintings of the London skyline, or perhaps the mast of a giant sailing ship passing along the river. English Heritage, on the other hand, were not keen, and said that it would be 'like a shard of glass through the heart of historic London' – thus inadvertently giving the building its name. It was officially opened on 5 July 2012, and currently hosts an observatory, three restaurants, two hotels, a television station, a business school, and office accommodation for numerous private companies.

Inside the station the number of terminating platforms was reduced from nine to six, while new through platforms were added, long enough to accommodate twelve-car trains if required. From 2016 the area underneath the raised platforms has been opened up and revamped into a modern concourse with shops, cafés, new entrances and exits. The concourse is Britain's biggest, and larger than the pitch at Wembley Stadium, for the first time enabling access to all the platforms from one place, and helping to end London Bridge Station's long-standing reputation for a frustrating and confusing travel experience for the 54 million commuters and tourists who pass through annually. Colonel Landmann would no doubt be amazed to see how his modest little station has developed over the past 180 years, although he would still recognize his iconic viaduct as it snakes away towards Greenwich. ✧

Chapter 2

EUSTON, 1837

OFTEN CONSIDERED THE FATHER OF railways, George Stephenson, together with his son Robert, were appointed engineers to the London and Birmingham Railway Company (LBRC), which was incorporated under an Act of Parliament and granted royal assent on 6 May 1833. The company made history by being the first to build a railway between two cities anywhere in the world.

The London and Birmingham Railway Company

Euston Station was the London terminus of the London and Birmingham Railway Company, and its story begins with a man often considered the father of railways, George Stephenson, together with his son Robert. They were appointed engineers to the London and Birmingham Railway Company, which was given parliamentary approval on 6 May 1833. The company was to create history as being the first to build a railway line from a major city to London, and Euston was to be the first 'inter-city' railway station ever to be built in any capital city in the world.

All new railways needed the approval of Parliament, and the first Bill proposing the new line and terminus at Euston was rejected by the House of Lords in 1832. However, a second attempt citing a terminus at Chalk Farm was successful, and the Act was passed on 6 May 1833. In the meantime, a revised compensation package for those whose land would be affected meant that Robert Stephenson could extend the line to Euston Grove as originally intended, and this was agreed by Parliament on 3 July 1835. The plan was that the LBRC would share a joint station with the Great Western Railway, who would run the western half of the station.

The chosen site was originally a large farm called 'Rhodes Farm' owned by the ancestors of Cecil Rhodes, Prime Minister of the Cape Colony in the 1890s and founder of Rhodesia, now Zimbabwe. The land was close to an estate owned by the Fitzroy family, the Dukes of Grafton, whose family seat was Euston Hall in Suffolk. Indeed, the name 'Euston' was already being used in place names in the area, such as Euston Road, Euston Square and Euston Grove, so 'Euston Station' was the name chosen for the new terminus.

Opening in 1830, the Liverpool to Manchester Railway was a wonderful development, being the first steam-powered railway between two cities. But it was only thirty miles long and covered relatively easy ground. Robert Stephenson's new railway from London to Birmingham would be just over 112 miles long, and to construct it to his exacting standards (a railway of easy gradients and imperceptible curves, over five high ridges and as many valleys) was a completely different matter. It was also an expensive one, and the company raised £2.5 million by selling shares in order to pay for it. The idea was met with violent opposition in parliament, with Sir Astley Cooper saying: 'Your scheme is preposterous in the extreme. It is of so extravagant a character as to be positively absurd.' But Stevenson was aware of his responsibilities and did not take his job lightly. It is said that he rode the whole length of the proposed route between London and Birmingham over twenty times before deciding on the best path to take.

The Early Euston Station

When the station opened on 20 July 1837 Queen Victoria had only just become queen in June of that year. This was the start of the Victorian Age, when new inventions were changing lives, and the landscape of Britain was about to be transformed as the railways began to take hold. The vision for Euston Station was that it was to be London's gateway to the Midlands, the North of England, and to Scotland. However, when the station opened it was a fairly basic affair, and the line only took you as far as Boxmoor in Hertfordshire. The complete line to Birmingham was not completed until September 1838.

There were only two platforms in the early Euston station, one each for arrivals and departures, with a couple of lines in between for storing carriages. These were partially covered by a fairly plain wrought-iron roof. The train shed itself was designed by Charles Fox, who specialized in railway design, and had invented the system of railway points in 1832. He was very experienced, and his company built the Crystal Palace in Hyde Park for the Great Exhibition of

1851 – but Euston was no glittering palace. The train shed was 200 feet long, unremarkable, and simply built to do the job.

Its practical amenities were quite modest. Being the first of its kind there was no other city terminus from which to take inspiration. When the station opened the central approach road was not ready, so passengers entered by a side entrance in Seymour Street from the east, or Melton Street from the west. For such an ambitious station there was a feeling that it was unfinished and deficient.

To add to the sense of anti-climax, regular steam engines were not powerful enough to pull the train carriages up the steep 1-in-77 incline out of the station. Instead they were initially hauled up the mile-long Camden bank by continuous ropes at the rate of twenty miles per hour. The ropes were pulled by two sixty-horsepower winding engines built by engineering firm Maudsley, Sons and Field, and positioned in an engine house in Camden. When a train was ready to leave the station the train was pushed by the station staff to the end of the Departure Parade, where the haulage rope was attached. A blast of air was sent along a pneumatic tube, which sounded a trumpet inside the engine house, creating what some said was a 'melancholic mysterious moaning', and the rope would be set in motion. A locomotive would then be attached to the train once it had been pulled up the incline.

Trains going the other way were allowed to free-wheel down the incline into the station with a brakesman, known as a 'bankrider', controlling the speed with the brakes, preventing the carriages from exceeding ten miles per hour. This system continued until July 1844 when locomotives were finally introduced, although a second 'pilot' engine was sometimes used to help get the carriages up the slope. The Camden engine house still exists today as flats, and can be seen in Gloucester Avenue, Primrose Hill.

Euston's Landmark Entrance

In marked contrast to the unimpressive train shed, the LBRC decided to create a landmark, an impressive entrance to the station, which would show the world what an important station Euston was, an edifice that symbolized the opening of a new era. Philip Hardwick's huge, Greek-style Doric arch, or propylaeum, was installed as the monumental entrance to the station, and immediately appeared rather incongruous. It stood away from the main train shed across a square courtyard, and facing out on to Drummond Street. Sometimes called a 'portico', it was the entrance to the land owned by the company, rather than to the station itself.

The huge, grey stone structure appeared out of proportion to the rest of the station buildings. It included a room in the roof, which could be reached by a spiral stairway in one corner of the structure, and was used to store drawings and surveys of the line. Adjacent to each side of the arch was a lodge building, with two further lodges either side, a short distance apart and linked by wrought-iron gates bearing the coat-of-arms of the LBRC. The four lodges with the arch in the centre were undoubtedly an impressive sight, though many thought these buildings simple and naive and with no real purpose, just a clumsy attempt to make a statement.

There was no doubt that the station looked a bit odd and disjointed. The arch was impressive, but it could also be seen as an embarrassment. This feeling was captured by author and lawyer Samuel Sidney in his 1851 book *Rides*

The Great Hall, Euston Station. MT124/88

on Railways, where he wrote that the railway passenger yard at Euston was best visited at 6am and seen by the grey light of a spring morning:

It is so still, so open; the tall columns of the portico entrance look down on you so grimly; the front of the booking-offices, in their garment of clean stucco look so primly respectable that you cannot help feeling ashamed of yourself – feeling as uncomfortable as when you have called too early on an economically genteel couple, and been shown into a handsome drawing room, on a frosty day, without a fire.

At seventy feet the arch was twice as high as its neighbouring lodges, and included four Doric columns, each of which was 27 feet 6 inches in height, built from Bramley Falls course-grained Yorkshire sandstone. The columns were hollow in the centre and built in sections, or courses, each course constructed from four separate quarter-pieces of stone. The triangular top section, or cornice, was originally decorated with projecting lions' heads, but these were removed in 1889 as they were not carved from Bramley Falls stone, and were not wearing very well. The arch was completed in May 1838 and cost £35,000 to build, and as far as the company was concerned it stood as a symbol of a new age of travel, on the edge of London, as a 'Gateway to the North'; it also signposted the LBRC as a solid, reliable provider of travel services.

Buildings and Services

Other buildings on the large site included a long, thin building running parallel to the platforms, with Greek-style columns, and a larger building used as a booking office, which again included classical columns. The accommodation was initially concentrated on the eastern side of the site, allowing room for the Great Western Railway to use the other half for their terminus. But the GWR's insistence on using broad-gauge track,

and various other difficulties, meant that they withdrew and built their terminus at Paddington.

Services at Euston Station developed quickly, and in 1838 a travelling Post Office train began running nightly at 8.30pm for Aberdeen, picking up and dropping mail as it sped along its 540-mile route. In the same year the LBRC relocated its offices from Cornhill to Euston, and in 1839 the Victoria and Euston Hotels were opened on the site. They were positioned forward of, and either side of the arch, creating a more dignified entrance to the station as a whole.

Until the 1850s Euston was the only London terminus for trains from the Midlands and the North, and as more and more railway companies began to use the lines to Euston it became obvious that expansion was necessary. One problem was that the platforms were too short, and some longer trains would block the lines for other trains waiting to leave. Front carriages often overlapped the end of the platforms, and engines occasionally stood in advance of their starting signals, with parcels having to be loaded on to the leading luggage van from the ballast. Finally in 1846 the decision was taken that redevelopment should take place, and George Carr Glyn, Chairman of the LBRC, is quoted as announcing to the Board, 'We have been obliged

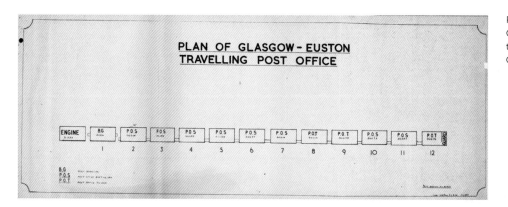

Plan of the Glasgow–Euston travelling Post Office. HO287/1496

to buy streets – streets, gentlemen – to give the public the accommodation they require.'

The Great Hall

In 1846 the LBRC amalgamated with the Grand Junction, and Manchester and Birmingham Railways, to form the London and North Western Railway (LNWR). New offices and meeting rooms were proposed at Euston, including the Great Hall, which opened to the public on 27 May 1849 and proved itself to be a unique masterpiece of Victorian genius. Designed by Philip Charles Hardwick (son of Philip, the designer of the arch) and built by William Cubitt and Company, the Great Hall was in effect a large waiting room, and at 126 feet long, 61 feet wide and 64 feet high it was the biggest one at the time in Britain.

The ceiling was said to be copied from the Basilica of St Paul-outside-the-Walls, in Rome: it was very ornate with no central supporting columns, and the largest of its kind in the world. The ceiling was coffered – that is, it consisted of a series of large panels, bearing various ornamental designs, the borders of which sprang from enormous, elaborately designed brackets, supported upon lions' heads, all round the upper half of the hall. The mouth of each lion held a ring by which were suspended beautifully arranged bunches of fruit and flowers. There were large square windows close to the roof on the eastern and western sides, and access to the company's upper rooms was via a grand, double-curved stone staircase leading to a balcony that ran around the hall.

The Shareholders' Room was reached via a large door at the top of the stairs, between a double row of columns. It gave the impression of being the 'Holy of Holies', only accessible by the High Priest of the company, and other shareholders,

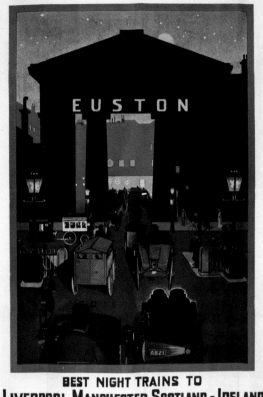

London and North Western Railway poster by Douglas Brown, 1905. COPY1/229B

of course. Over the door was an exceedingly bold and elegantly designed bas-relief by the sculptor John Thomas featuring the figure of a seated Britannia, supported on her right by a life-sized figure representing the Arts and Sciences, and on the left by the Roman God Mercury, with her arm resting on the head of a large lion.

The walls of the Great Hall included eight panels in bas-relief, two in each corner, also the work of John Thomas. They were placed high up near the ceiling in the corners of the Hall, and represented the eight major towns and counties served by the LNWR: Northampton,

Lancashire, Birmingham, London, Chester, Carlisle, Manchester and Liverpool. Each panel featured three characters – a man, a woman and a child – together with a building representative of the town or area concerned.

The total cost of building the Hall was £122,532. The walls were of cement, decorated to look like granite, and the lateral columns were painted as red granite, with white marble bases and capitals. It is said that the great Victorian painter and sculptor George Frederic Watts offered to decorate the Hall with a series of frescoes free of charge, illustrating the 'Progress of the Cosmos', but the directors refused, saying that the paintings would be ruined by fog and smoke – a real possibility, considering the amount of dirt created by steam trains and a persistently smoking public. Apparently the offer was made on condition that the company paid for the scaffolding and paint, but the directors declined since they had no funds for such a purpose. One critic suggested that the directors simply preferred 'money-making ugliness'. There is no mention of the Watts offer in the company minutes, so the whole story may be apocryphal.

To the east and west of the Great Hall were booking halls, which in 1912 were converted to refreshment rooms. Originally lit by gas lamps, electric lighting was installed in 1927, the Hall being 'flood-lit' at night with high powered lamps fitted beneath the windows. By 1854 a large white marble statue of George Stephenson had been placed at the foot of the central staircase leading to the Board Room. The fifteen-foot statue was created by Edward Hodges Baily, who also sculpted the statue of Nelson at the top of his column in Trafalgar Square.

In the Annual Meeting Room there was a bust of Henry Booth, Secretary of the Liverpool and Manchester Railway, the man who suggested to Stephenson the idea of the multi-tubular boiler, which ensured the success of the 'The Rocket' engine. He invented the screw coupling, which linked carriages together, and was an advocate of universal time across Britain to aid in the preparation of railway timetables. It was not until 1847 that the Post Office agreed to universal time across the country, and the railways adopted Greenwich Meantime across the network. Prior to this a passenger setting his watch and travelling from Euston to Birmingham in the 1830s would find that by the time he reached Harrow

Day School for Boys and Girls

The LNWR, like many other railway companies, tried to promote loyalty and cohesiveness amongst its staff, and as part of this approach a Day School for Boys and Girls was set up at Euston Station in 1853. The purpose of the school was to provide the children of employees with a good, sound and practical education amongst large, well ventilated school rooms at No. 65 Seymour Street. A wide range of subjects was taught, including mensuration, composition, mapping and needlework for the girls, as well as reading, grammar and arithmetic. The school fees ranged from 2d to 6d per week, depending on the wages of the parent. In 1871 the number of children on the books of the school was 220 boys and 180 girls, although the average attendance in March of that year was only 201 per day. This was due in part to a smallpox epidemic, when infected children were not permitted to attend, but also because many families had been forced out of their homes as local houses had been demolished to make way for new railway buildings.

he would be one minute ahead of local time, and on reaching Birmingham he would find the clocks 7¼ minutes slower than his London set watch.

Further Development

The station building continued to evolve during the late nineteenth century. The company's engineer, William Baker, arranged for a large part of the roof over platforms three, five and six to be raised by six feet in 1870 by hoisting up the supporting columns and inserting octagonal cast-iron pedestals underneath them. Hydraulic power was used to complete the work, which lasted for only one week, and the station remained open throughout. It is said that the whole roof was raised without breaking a single pane of glass.

Then in 1880 the two separate hotels were joined together by a new united building known as the Euston Hotel – East Wing and West Wing, which unfortunately obliterated the view of the Arch from the Euston Road. Italian-born French sculptor Baron Carlo Marochetti created a bronze statue of Robert Louis Stephenson for the Institution of Civil Engineers with the intention of placing it in St Margaret's Gardens, Parliament Square. However, this situation was reserved for statesmen, so the statue was put away in the cellars of the Institution until 1871 when it was presented to the LNWR, and placed between two of the entrance lodges in Euston Square. The statue is almost twice life-size and stands on a red-marble base, inscribed with the dates of his birth and death. It can still be seen today in the new Euston Station forecourt.

Continued development meant that by 1891 the station had grown to eighteen acres. More platforms had been built, and there was now a suite of rooms for the royal family and other special passengers. A new signal box was added in 1891, the largest of its kind, with 288 levers (including thirty-three spare ones) controlling the signals and points.

One foggy afternoon in 1916 the Great Hall at Euston became an impromptu music hall, when the world-famous Swiss 'King of Clowns' Grock, together with comedian Fred Emney, happened to be passing through. Passengers were becoming restless as their trains were delayed by the fog, and so a piano was wheeled out from the shareholders' room on to the balcony at the head of the stairs, and the comic duo, dressed in their respective costumes of a French clown and an 'Old Lady getting over a stile', staged a spontaneous musical comedy show, which had travellers roaring with laughter at their antics.

Euston Station in World War I

During World War I railway employees made a huge contribution to the war effort, both in terms of railway work in northern France, and as general servicemen. In honour of their sacrifice Field Marshal Earl Haig unveiled the LNWR war memorial, designed by the company's architect Wynn Owen, on 21 October 1921, a striking and dignified monument to the 3,719 employees of the company who gave their lives in the Great War. Located in the main approach to Euston Station, the memorial is an obelisk carved from Portland stone, forty-five feet high and featuring a cross and wreath on each side. At the base four bronze figures, each weighing one ton, stand with heads bowed, representing the Navy, the Infantry, the Artillery and the Royal Flying Corps. On the southern face of the monument an inscription reads: 'In Memory of our Glorious Dead'. The obelisk is intentionally plain, devoid of superfluous decoration, a memorial to the fallen, and in no way a celebration of victory.

Earl Haig, in his address at the unveiling, drew attention to the debt owed by the Army during the war 'to the railways of this country, and not least among them to this great Company to which you belong, for their splendid conduct and loyal support throughout that mighty struggle.' What the railwaymen managed to achieve is indeed staggering. In 1918 alone the railwaymen of the British Army constructed 2,340 miles of broad-gauge track and 1,348 miles of narrow-gauge railway, which carried 530,000 tons of men and equipment to and from the front lines. A total of 1,200 locomotives and 52,600 trucks were employed – a railway system built in one year equal in size to the Great Central Railway at the time, and nearly twice as big as the London, Brighton and South Coast Railway.

The LNWR provided a total of 31,742 men who joined the armed forces, which represents one-third of the company workforce. Of those who joined up, 11.7 per cent lost their lives. Naval and military honours were secured by 950 employees, and three men were awarded the Victoria Cross: Private W. Wood, Private E. Sykes and Lance-Corporal J. A. Christie.

In the early days of World War I, a buffet was opened at Euston station for the benefit of sailors and soldiers when travelling. The LNWR gave a room free of charge, and it was staffed by volunteers who served up to 45,000 free meals per month to soldiers and sailors passing through. In December 1917 Sir Gilbert Claughton, the Chairman of the Company, made a public appeal through the *Evening Standard* newspaper on behalf of the buffet, raising a sum of £12,500. The buffet ran until 5 July 1919, when it closed, leaving a balance in hand of nearly £2,000. Since the buffet was a registered charity, the Charity Commissioners decided that the remaining money should be given away in the form of grants to widows, dependants and orphans of railway employees killed or incapacitated during the war.

One such beneficiary was railway clerk H. R. Boasten, who was born on 14 March 1891 and entered service with the LNWR in 1906, based at Luton. He joined the army in August 1914 and went to France in the RAMC, and was mentioned in Despatches for Meritorious Service. In September 1917 he was given a commission as captain in the Royal Flying Corps – but in April 1918 his aeroplane met with a collision in the air.

As a result of the crash the right side of his face was smashed, he suffered head injuries, and his right arm was broken. He was demobbed in 1920, but his arm had not been set properly and he never fully recovered the use of it. He felt that he could no longer undertake clerical work for the LNWR, nor was he able to carry out manual work. His facial operations, which took place in a private nursing home, were expensive, and he was having difficulty paying his bills. Although receiving a Disability Pension of £100 per year from the government, he was forced at the age of thirty to apply to the LNWR Superannuation Committee for his company pension, and under a separate application received a grant of £40 from the Soldiers and Sailors Euston Free Buffet Fund, being one of many railwaymen who experienced tremendous medical and financial difficulties following World War I, through no fault of their own.

Organizational Changes in the 1920s

In the 1920s there were large organizational changes for Euston station. In 1922 electric trains were used for the first time between Euston and Watford, to accommodate commuter traffic to and from London. In 1923, most railway companies in Great Britain were grouped together into four large companies – known as the Big Four – and the LNWR was absorbed into the London, Midland and Scottish Railway (LMS). The LMS in the 1930s wanted to replace the whole of Euston Station, and plans were drawn up to include new blocks of flats to accommodate 588 'working class' people. The flats would be required to house the people relocated when the new station was reconstructed and expanded. However, the intervention of World War II, and the relative poverty of the newly nationalized railway of 1948, further delayed any major reconstruction.

Euston Station in the 1950s

Life at Euston Station during the 1950s was fairly humdrum. By 1954 over 430 trains used the station every day, providing services to 50,000 long distance travellers and 20,000 suburban passengers. The tracks had been redesigned into a simpler format allowing faster movement in and out of the station, and the platforms had been lengthened to allow for longer trains. There were a few occasions when publicity was courted, such as in December 1954 when the Great Hall was once again used as a venue for entertainment in the form of a Christmas carol concert given by the staff of British Railways London Midland Region.

In 1957 the red carpet was laid out for Oliver Lyttelton, 1st Viscount Chandos, to mark the arrival of a new type of diesel electric locomotive to be used to haul freight trains. Lord Chandos, Chairman of the electrical engineering company

Associated Electrical Industries, arrived carrying a rolled umbrella, and was ceremoniously handed a golden key before clambering aboard the box-like engine along with Lord Rusholme, Chairman of the London Midland Area Board of British Railways. Both men hung their homburgs on a couple of handy hooks and rumbled along for a few yards whilst a penetrating fanfare blasted out from a two-tone klaxon. At the end of the platform the engine halted for photographs, then the engine trundled back to the red carpet again, and the station master completed the ceremony by doffing his top hat.

In 1955 a new lounge bar was launched at Euston called the Royal Scot Bar, replacing the former First Class Bar. Waitresses served light meals and special grills, and passengers could choose from twenty-four different kinds of beer. The bar was located next to the existing cafeteria, which served 800 meals and 3,600 cups of tea or coffee daily, and was part of the British Transport Commission's country-wide catering improvement scheme. These rather low-key highlights are indicative of the slow evolution of the station's life through the 1950s.

A New Euston Station

Finally in 1959, after years of planning, the decision was taken to knock down the complex of century-old buildings and replace them with a shiny new station, one that was efficient and worthy of the twentieth century. The contract was awarded in 1961, and due to the restricted floorplan of the original station, any expansion could only succeed by building over the area occupied by those symbols of Victorian pioneering inventiveness: the Great Hall and the Doric arch. It seemed that both would need to be demolished.

The demolition of Euston Station, 1961. ZLIB4/404

It was going to be a controversial and unpopular decision, and there was much discussion between the London County Council and the British Transport Commission, neither of whom wanted the expense of preserving the Great Hall or the iconic Arch, while equally neither of them wanted the blame for knocking them down. The Minister of Housing and Local Government hoped that the Minister of Transport would make the announcement in parliament, and thereby become 'answerable'.

A wide-ranging appeal to save the Arch was set in motion. Some wanted to relocate it elsewhere, others wanted to incorporate it into the new station, and a Canadian company even offered to relocate the Arch for £90,000. A deputation met with Prime Minister Harold Macmillan on 24 October 1961, headed by Sir Charles Wheeler, President of the Royal Academy and other high profile supporters, including Sir John Betjeman, poet and Chairman of the Victorian Society. They each stated their case as to why the Arch must be preserved, although some complained afterwards that Macmillan listened with his eyes closed throughout the meeting. Betjeman also wrote directly to Macmillan, yet despite these efforts the fate of the monument was sealed.

The Minister of Transport, Ernest Marples, claimed that the cost of moving the Arch would be £190,000, whereas the cost of demolishing it would be £12,000. Macmillan agreed, saying that dismantling the Arch and relocating it, even if somewhere could be found for it – one suggestion was on the roundabout on the Euston Road – would be expensive and would delay the building of the new station. Macmillan summarized his reasons for sanctioning the demolition in an apologetic letter sent to Wheeler on 2 November, the text of which was issued to the Press the following day. The demolition started almost immediately, and the Arch was gone by the end of 1961.

The new station heralded the electric age of railway travel when it was opened by Queen Elizabeth II on 14 October 1968. Gone was the scattered collection of heavy-looking stone buildings, haunted by steam and soot. Instead the public were greeted by a sleek, new low-rise building of concrete and glass. Designed by committee, the new Euston Station was modern, functional and efficient, with a parcels depot built above the eighteen platforms, a long, wide concourse and ticket hall, shops and food outlets.

A proposed setting for the Euston Arch. HLG126/885

The London County Council refused to allow shops and offices to be built above Euston on the grounds that it would become too congested. But with fifteen acres of flat roof, people complained that it had the feeling of a modern airport, lacking the quirky, curious charm of the old station, replaced instead by a soulless low-lying, nationalized, generic public construction. But then stations are not built to amuse, but to enable efficient travel, and this was not the last transformation that Euston would see.

It is ironic that the original station buildings, regarded by many as symbols of timeless quality, were swept away and replaced by a 'modern' 1960s minimalist block, which itself now looks tired and dated. Students of architecture study Euston Station if they want to see how buildings were built fifty years ago. Today Euston is London's sixth busiest station, and further development is likely, particularly as it is a contender to be the London terminus of the planned High Speed 2 (HS2) line to the North. ✸

Architect's drawing of Euston Station from Eversholt Street, in the 1960s. AN193/54

Chapter 3

FENCHURCH STREET, 1840

The Thomas Briggs Murder

Fenchurch Street Station has an unfortunate connection with the first ever murder on the railways in Britain. The unhappy victim was a sixty-nine-year-old City banker named Thomas Briggs, who happened to be in the wrong place at the wrong time. He boarded a train at Fenchurch Street at about 9.45pm on 9 July 1864. By the time the train had reached Hackney Wick, a distance of just under nine miles, he had been robbed, badly beaten about the head and thrown from the train. His brutal attacker was Franz Müller, a German national who worked as a tailor and who chose his target at random. Although Briggs was still alive when he was found on the tracks, he was so badly beaten that he died later from his injuries.

It seems that the motive for Müller's attack was the need for money to help pay for his planned emigration to America. Having taken items from Briggs he later sold them to a jeweller, who contacted the police with a description of the man. Müller lost no time in leaving England on a sailing ship called the *Victoria*, but the police were on to him and gave chase in a faster steam ship, *The City of Manchester*. They were waiting for him when he reached New York.

Extradited back to Britain, Müller was tried at the Old Bailey and sentenced to death, and

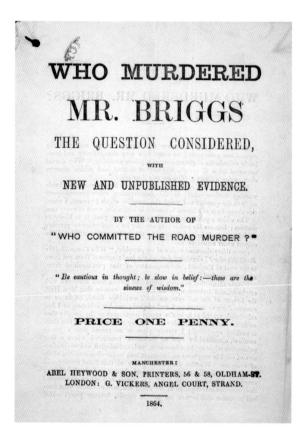

'Who murdered Thomas Briggs' leaflet, printed in 1864. MEPO3/76

executed by public hanging outside Newgate Prison on 14 November 1864. He was only twenty-four years old. The case led to a number of changes in the law and helped to bring about improvements in the design of railway carriages, such as the introduction of communication cords, and the redesigning of carriages with corridors, which allowed passengers to move between compartments so they were no longer isolated from fellow travellers during their journeys.

The London and Blackwall Railway (L&BR)

The history of Fenchurch Street Station starts with the Commercial Railway, which was approved by Parliament on 28 July 1836 to provide a short 3½ mile railway line from the Minories station, near the Tower of London, to Blackwall and the East and West India Docks. John Rennie was appointed as the company's Chief Engineer. At the same time George Stephenson also submitted a rival application for his London & Blackwall Railway and Steam Navigation Depot Company, but this scheme was rejected by Parliament, so planning for the Commercial Railway went ahead. It wasn't long, however, before the company experienced financial difficulties, and it was soon taken over by Stephenson's rival company. Both schemes had a similar aim, which was to benefit from the commercial traffic generated by the docks, and the frequent journeys made by individual people between the River Thames and the City of London.

The prospectus of the new railway described their principal aims as being the conveyance of goods from the East and West India Docks, and the landing and despatch of coal cargoes, allowing ships to unload at this part of the Thames without having to risk damage, delays and congestion by going further up the river. They also wanted to profit from regular passenger traffic, which currently used roads or the river. They estimated that 4,300 people travelled each day to the docks by coach or by horse-bus, each paying 6d for the forty-minute journey. Those who went by riverboat seldom spent less than an hour on the 6½ mile circuitous trip around the Isle of Dogs. So the new railway company proposed to charge the same fare as the horse-bus, but to cut down the journey time from the City to the docks to only ten minutes.

The new line opened on 6 July 1840, having been engineered by Robert Stephenson following John Rennie's original plan. At the same time the company changed its name to the London and Blackwall Railway (L&BR). The opening Ceremony for the line was held at the Minories station, and it was a typically lavish Victorian occasion with 1,500 invited guests, MPs and officials gathered in the booking hall. At twelve o'clock a band played, while the railway guards in smart blue and white uniforms conducted the first party to the new train. The carriages were pushed along the line by servants of the company for the first twenty yards before the hauling mechanism carried them down the track. Eye-witness reports state that the inhabitants of two dilapidated tenements took the tiles off the roofs and stuck their heads through the holes to get a good view of the train as it trundled past. By 3pm all the guests had been taken to Blackwall Station where they enjoyed a sumptuous dinner of turtle, whitebait, grouse with claret, jelly and ice, washed down with coffee and liqueurs, all supplied by Mr Lovegrove, proprietor of the nearby Brunswick Hotel.

The hotel, with its associated pub the Brunswick Tavern, was situated at the western end of Brunswick Wharf, and had a reputation for fine dining. According to a contemporary journalist writing in 1840, it attracted both the gourmet and the gourmand (glutton), both of whom would enjoy 'the peculiar delicacy of whitebait with the luxurious accompaniment of cold punch. And thither, by aid of the Blackwall Railway, he may be wafted in ten minutes'. The writer also recommended a turn or two on the terrace by the pier, 'there being nothing more repellent of dyspepsia than a river breeze'.

The original stations on the line were at Minories, Shadwell, Stepney, Lime House, West India Docks, Poplar and Blackwall. From Minories to West India Docks the line was carried on a brick viaduct of 285 arches for 2½ miles, followed by an embankment, before finally reaching Poplar and Blackwall through a shallow cutting. The Minories station was the intended London terminus, but the company found that it was too far from the City, and a new terminus was planned for Lime Street. The Corporation of London turned this down, but approved a further application for a terminus at Fenchurch Street, which went ahead and opened on 29 July 1841.

The L&BR's Unusual Features

The actual L&BR railway line was unusual for two reasons. Firstly the line was cable hauled, each of its two tracks running a seven-mile continuous hemp rope powered by stationary steam engines at each end of the line, which drove drums like large cotton reels. The drums would alternately wind in the rope for the length of one complete journey, and then let it out again for the return trip. Once the rope was in motion it did not stop until the leading carriages reached the end of the line. Train carriages would move by gripping the moving rope, known as 'pinning', and on reaching a station the rope would be released, called 'slipping'. All of this was controlled by

a guard operating leavers connected to iron grips beneath the carriage, similar to a modern cable-car.

When Fenchurch Street was constructed a quarter of a mile beyond the Minories it was built on a rising gradient of 1 in 150 so that carriages could be slipped from the rope at Minories and allowed to coast up the short slope into the new station by momentum alone. Trains starting out from Fenchurch Street would be pushed along by station staff until gravity pulled them down on to the rope-powered track at Minories.

The same sloping arrangement was built at the Blackwall terminus at the other end of the track. When the train was ready to start, the guard at the London end called up his colleague at Blackwall on an electric telegraph 'enclosed in a neat mahogany case', and the station masters at the intermediate stations were also informed. The Blackwall engine drum would start to wind in the rope, and as each station was reached the appropriate carriages were detached, while the rest of the train continued.

In January 1838 engineers George Stephenson and G. P. Bidder submitted a detailed report to the directors of the company on two options, spelling out the advantages of the rope system over locomotives. Basically, they explained that the rope system would enable faster travel between stations (which were actually fairly close together) without the inconvenience and expense of manning and maintaining locomotives. Locomotives would also require four lines of track to be built, and would need maintenance areas and facilities for them, whereas the rope system would only require two lines of track and therefore the width, height and cost of the viaduct would all be much reduced. It would be a quieter, cleaner and cheaper system to build and to run. Local objections to railway nuisances such as noise, whistles, steam and ash deposits would be avoided, and as an example of how quiet stationary engines could be the report states that 'at Camden Station, you may actually stand immediately over the engines while in full work, and yet be ignorant of their vicinity'.

The rope system was not ideal, however, as it often became twisted or stretched, and would usually break completely once or twice per month. Stephenson was at a loss as to what was causing the problem. He speculated that the reason might be that it was being coiled over the drum at the Minories, but under the drum at Blackwall, or that the left-hand or right-hand twist in the rope might play a part, so both types were tried, but this made little difference. Even a metal wire cable was introduced in 1841, but this caused more problems due to continual kinking, and the additional weight of the cable itself.

The second unusual feature of the L&BR line was that it used a very obscure 5ft ½in track gauge, a type of broad gauge used by only two other railway companies in Britain. Track widths were not prescribed at this time, and a railway company could choose to use any width, within reason. It is thought that they chose a broad gauge in anticipation of the freight that they planned to carry from the docks. However, in 1849 a new line extension was opened linking to the Eastern Counties Railway (ECR) at Bow, and it therefore became necessary to replace the broad-gauge track with the standard gauge of 4ft 8½in. At the same time the rope traction system was abandoned in favour of steam engines, both of which enabled ECR trains to use the track.

Trains ran every fifteen minutes, and the fare was 6d for first class and 4d for third class. The blue and gold-painted rolling stock comprised first class coaches, first and third class composites, and third class carriages known as 'Stanhopes'. Civil engineer and writer on railways Francis Whishaw wrote of them in his book *Railways of Great Britain and Ireland* (1842):

> We were astonished to see several most respectfully dressed persons riding in the Stanhope compartments, which are intended especially for those who cannot afford to pay for better accommodation.

He also complained that the first class coaches did not include elbows (armrests) between the seats, 'which would sometimes be exceedingly convenient to keep one aloof from an unpleasant fellow-traveller…the journey is, however, but of short duration.'

The Minories station was small and basic, although there was a siding in which seven coaches could stand, and a platform twenty-five feet wide for unloading goods. The platform was fitted with a crane and a trap door so that recently received goods could be lowered directly on to carts in the street below. Two other trap doors were fitted with shutes, allowing bagged or bailed goods to be slid down into storage rooms. It is recorded that in 1854 the station was handling 100 tons of goods per day.

Fenchurch Street Station Design

Fenchurch Street Station is not actually in Fenchurch Street but in nearby London Street and Fenchurch Place, a short road constructed especially to serve the station. It was designed by the L&BR engineer (Sir) George Berkeley, who specialized in foreign railways. The station opened on 29 July 1841, and from a rather

Drawing of the train shed at Fenchurch Street Station. ZSPC11/347

slow start passenger numbers gradually increased to make it a compact but busy little station.

Fenchurch Street was initially built with two platforms, and three additional ones were built in 1854 to accommodate the increased traffic from the ECR and the NLR. The front of the building was built from yellow stock bricks, topped with a curved pediment that matched the arc of the main iron and glass train-shed roof, which stretched 300 feet along the platforms with an overall span of 105 feet in width. On the ground floor were two separate booking offices, one for the L&BR and the other for the LTSR services, and two staircases led up to the small passenger concourse and the platforms. The front entrance was, and still is, plain, neat and tidy, with only the central clock and the undulating wooden canopy providing additional decoration.

Passenger Trade

During the summer months steam ships would leave Blackwall Pier taking day-trippers to Herne Bay and Margate. These were complemented by the Watermen Company's steamers bringing passengers from London's West End to Blackwall. The L&BR started to run its own steamers, and from Blackwall Pier you could travel as far as Rotterdam, Holland and Antwerp in Belgium. Between 1854 and 1858 various agreements were reached with other railway companies, which enabled passengers to travel from Fenchurch Street to Tilbury and Southend. The station also became a terminus for the North London Railway (NLR) coming in from the west, and the London Tilbury and Southend Railway (LTSR), which developed new lines benefiting from the

THE ILLUSTRATED LONDON NEWS [Dec. 10, 1853

NEW TERMINUS OF THE BLACKWALL RAILWAY, AT FENCHURCH-STREET.

RAIL 1005/477

LONDON AND BLACKWALL RAILWAY.—ENLARGE-
MENT OF THE FENCHURCH-STREET STATION.

The growing importance of the London and Blackwall Railway, the
immense number of passengers passing through its London terminus,
and the increase anticipated from the working arrangements of the
company with the Eastern Counties and Tilbury and Southend Railways, have for some time made it apparent that an enlargement of the
Fenchurch-street Station would be necessary.

For several months past the works and buildings requisite to effect
this have been steadily progressing; and on Saturday, the 19th ult., a
portion of the new Station was opened to the public, and the whole will
be very shortly completed.

The new Station will comprise booking-offices and waiting-rooms,
with platform accommodation for the London and Blackwall, the North
London, the Eastern Counties, and the Tilbury and South-end Railways,
covered by one roof, 101 feet span, and upwards of 300 feet long; there
is also a wing, containing the secretary's, and other offices, and the board-
room.

Considerable care and judgment have been required in the execution
of the works to avoid any interruption to the traffic, which has been continued throughout the progress of the works. This circumstance, together with the difficulty in obtaining possession of the land, &c., have
caused considerable delay in the execution of the works.

The station has been built by Messrs. J. and C. Rigby, of Westminster; and the roof constructed by Messrs. C. J. Mare and Co.
of Blackwall, under the superintendence of Mr. George Berkely, the
Company's Engineer. RAIL 1005/477

Royal Albert Docks and new factories along the Thames.

Fenchurch Street saw rapid growth in annual passenger numbers, from seven million in 1861 to a peak of thirty-three million in 1903. Thereafter, however, numbers began to drop as the telephone replaced messengers travelling between the docks and the City, while trams and other railway lines drew passengers away. Much of the original Blackwall line finally closed in 1926, the route eventually being used by the Docklands Light Railway between Minories and Poplar, opening in 1987. By 1913 Fenchurch Street saw only around seventeen million passengers, with

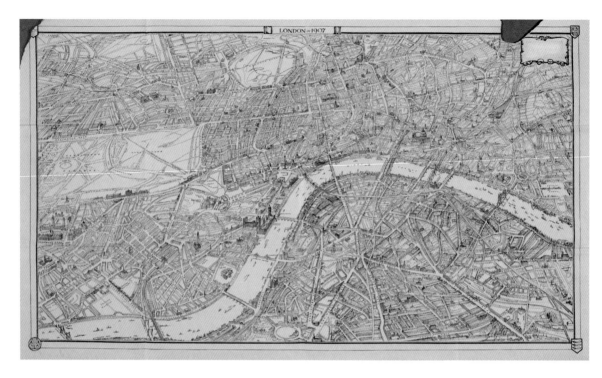

London in 1906; Fenchurch Street Station is visible just north of the Tower of London. COPY1/325

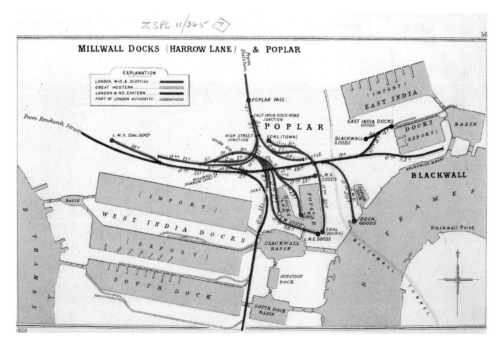

Millwall Docks.

ZSPC11/345

fifteen million in 1955, while currently it draws seventeen to eighteen million passengers per year.

It was the first mainline terminus to be located actually inside the City of London, although the area was rather run down and not particularly pleasant. A letter to the General Board of Health written in 1849 by Surgeon W. Cook calls attention to two streets near Trinity Square, namely Postern Row and Little George Street. He explains that these pavements have long been in 'a most disgraceful condition', with large holes receiving not only rainwater but 'offensive matter of other descriptions'. He complains that the state of these thoroughfares appears to him 'not only offensive to the eye and nose, but very injurious to health'. Cook also calls attention to a passage leading from Crutched Friars to Fenchurch Street: 'a great thoroughfare for pedestrians – but no decent person can pass through it without being annoyed by urinary and excrementitious deposits.'

Various railway company take-overs led up to an unusual situation where the station building was owned by one company while its services were being run by another rival company. This came about because the L&BR owned the station and they were taken over in 1866 by the Great Eastern Railway, which became part of the London and North Eastern Railway at the grouping in 1923. The main services, however, were run by the LTSR, which was taken over by the Midland Railway in 1912, which in turn became part of the London Midland and Scottish Railway at the grouping.

Derailments and Accidents

The approach tracks to the station were quite prone to derailments due to the necessity of having sharp curves through the narrow passages between buildings. In March 1882 an engine derailed outside the station, and on 24 October 1883 another engine was derailed twice on the same day at the same set of points just outside the station approaching platform number five. At 10.30am the engine was travelling at about 10 to 15 miles per hour when the driver said it appeared to jump off the rails on reaching the points, with the leading wheels ending up on the neighbouring track. At the same spot at 2.30pm the same engine, travelling more slowly this time, again jumped from the track, but luckily came to rest back on its own rails and continued into the station.

There were reports of similar accidents occurring on this stretch of track, and the Board of Trade's Accident Inspector, Major-General C. S. Hutchinson of the Royal Engineers, stated that the accidents were caused by the tightness of the curve. He recommended that the curve should only be approached at speeds of 5mph or less, and that the gauge of the rails should be increased slightly at this point to allow for flexibility of wheel movement on the rails.

A similar accident occurred the following February, in 1884. In this case the 8.37am passenger train from North Woolwich was entering the station when all the wheels of the engine left the rails at the sharp curve leading from the right-hand up-line to platform five, and only stopped after running about forty-nine yards. No one was injured, although the engine suffered some minor damage. On investigation Hutchinson found that the tracks had indeed been widened, and that a 5mph speed limit had been put in place. However, on interviewing the staff he heard a number of different versions of the truth. The driver stated that the train had not exceeded 5mph, but the fireman said that it was 'not much more than 5mph'. The front guard, however, said that the train had not exceeded 8mph, and the rear guard swore that the train was travelling between 8 and 10mph.

Hutchinson concluded that the train was probably travelling at twice the suggested speed, and that if his recommendations were followed in future there should be no more accidents of this type. Indeed, it was not until August 1890 that the next derailment occurred.

Reorganization

Between 1932 and 1935 the station was reorganized due to the fact that working capacity had been reached, and yet there was little room for physical expansion since the buildings either side of the tracks abutted them so closely. Two island platforms were installed, and the number of platforms was actually reduced from five to four, but the approach to the station was widened to four lines, providing independent access to each platform from any of the running lines. In order to achieve this, the corner of the Royal Mint Street East warehouse was moved back, and an engine turntable that had been recessed into the wall was completely removed. The concourse was opened up by relocating a bookstall and the telegraph office, and new platform barriers were installed, along with electric colour light signalling and automatic points.

World War II Shelter

During World War II, many stations were obliged to offer air-raid shelter accommodation for those using the railway. Fenchurch Street simply did not have the space inside the station, so in 1940 the Ministry of Home Security arranged for a surface shelter to be built on an adjacent site next to the nearby street of Crutched Friars. This was designed to cope with peak rush-hour traffic at the station; it was built from reinforced concrete, included thirteen entrances, and could accommodate 3,500 people. The building was the largest shelter in the area, covering 30,000 square feet. It originally included 140 chemical toilets, 140 buckets, and a consignment of hurricane lamps, although by 1943 sleeping accommodation had been installed along with water-borne sanitation.

Various problems regarding the construction and design of the building meant that contractors involved in the refurbishment of it were in dispute with the Corporation of London over costs, as it seems there was more wrong with the building than there was right. Nevertheless, during the months of October 1940 to March 1941 the shelter provided safe accommodation for passengers and others during a total of 280 air raids.

Improvements and Modernization

Between 1959 and 1962 the lines out of Fenchurch Street were electrified under British Rail, but the station began to acquire a bad reputation for uncleanliness and overcrowding. Some began to call it the 'Misery Line', although to be fair this name has been applied to several different railway lines in London at various different times.

In the 1980s the train shed was demolished and replaced by an 'air space' development above the platforms, providing offices set back from the historic Victorian frontage. These offices comprise a pyramidal structure in muted colours, giving the impression that they are behind the station rather than above it, blending in with similar modern office buildings surrounding the station. Five floors of prestige office space were built at a cost of £28 million, paid for by the Norwich Union Insurance Group, which took out a lease with British Rail.

At the same time the facilities in the station itself were rebuilt, with escalators replacing the stairs, and the shops and offices around the passenger concourse being updated. In July 1994 the station closed for seven weeks for works on the track and signalling system, while in 2013 a new entrance was created. In 2015 the rail company C2C, which currently operates services from the station, received the Passenger Operator of the Year award for their punctual services from Fenchurch Street and out through twenty-six stations to Shoeburyness in South Essex.

Fenchurch Street Today

Today Fenchurch Street remains the smallest of the London termini, almost deserted at weekends; it is mainly used by office workers from Essex during the morning and evening rush-hours. The poet John Betjeman used it for day trips to Southend and described it as 'a delightful hidden old terminus'. Tucked away in a back-street location, a low-rise Victorian station with a museum-piece frontage, it suffers from having no link to the London Underground, and unlike most other London termini it has never had an associated hotel. Nevertheless, continued commuter traffic to the tune of fifteen million passengers per year, albeit in concentrated bursts, means that its future is secure. ✧

Chapter 4

WATERLOO, 1848

FROM THE MID-1600S IMPORTING GOODS to Britain from abroad by ship was a slow and hazardous business. Having already navigated long distances from Britain's colonies they would then need to work their way along England's south coast, around Kent and along the Thames estuary to London, risking attack from Dutch vessels, and later the French, particularly during the Napoleonic wars, when ships were vulnerable in the English Channel. Mail and some goods on smaller vessels would be quickly landed at ports such as Falmouth in Cornwall, and then transported by road to London. But various schemes were devised to enable larger vessels, goods, merchants, and of course the Royal Navy to connect with London

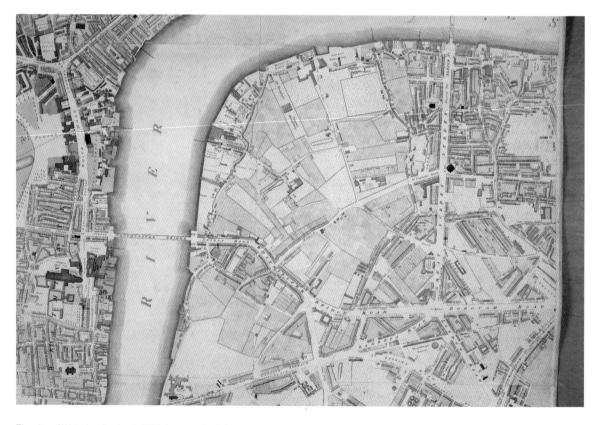

The site of Waterloo Station in 1799, in a map by R. Horwood. Note the open fields. MR1/682

more easily, preferably without having to get too close to the continent.

One idea proposed in 1803 by Sir John Rennie, the Scottish engineer who specialized in docks, bridges and canals, was to build a ship canal all the way from Portsmouth to London. The planned route would have been 100 miles in length, with forty-one locks, stretching from the Croydon Canal down to Portsmouth on the south coast. The canal was never actually built, but the coming of the railways brought new opportunities for communication with the south coast, and following surveys by engineer Francis Giles a new railway line linking London with the port city of Southampton was approved by Parliament in 1834: the London and South-ampton Railway (LSR).

The Route South: The London and Southampton Railway (LSR)

The LSR opened in sections between 1838 and 1840, and quickly became a popular and successful business; its aim was to connect the busy south coast port of Southampton with the capital, and to benefit from commercial business travelling in both directions. Its London terminus was originally at Nine Elms station in Battersea,

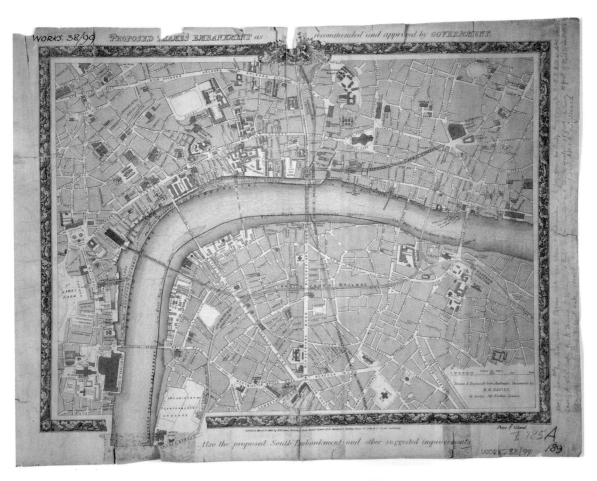

Map of the proposed Thames Embankment, showing the 'South Western Station' in 1862. WORK38/99

on the south bank of the Thames, which opened on 21 May 1838. At the same time the company broadened its audience by changing its name to the London and South Western Railway (LSWR). The route south took in stations at Wimbledon, Surbiton, Woking, Basingstoke and Winchester, and later on included lines to Windsor, Portsmouth and Salisbury. The opening of Nine Elms station was timed to coincide with the Epsom Derby, and it is said that 5,000 people arrived at the station looking forward to a day at the races.

Designed by Sir William Tite, architect and Member of Parliament, the Nine Elms station was located too far away from central London for passengers to complete their journeys easily, and they would have to travel on by road, or along the River Thames. The area of Nine Elms was a quiet, damp, boggy position prone to flooding, with osier beds of young willow trees grown for basket weaving, and it wasn't really suitable as a location for a mainline terminus. So in 1844 an Act was passed allowing the LSWR to extend the line by two miles and to build a new terminus closer to central London. This was called the Metropolitan Extension and construction started in July 1846, the line being extended north-eastwards, with a new intermediate station added at Vauxhall, and a new terminus built next to Waterloo Bridge. The old Nine Elms station was then closed to passenger traffic, and became a goods station.

Waterloo Bridge

Waterloo Bridge was originally going to be called 'Strand Bridge', but it opened on 18 June 1817, exactly two years after the Battle of Waterloo, so it was renamed Waterloo Bridge to commemorate the victory of the British, Dutch and Prussians over Napoleon's French army in 1815. The bridge was designed by John Rennie, and was much narrower than the bridge we know today. By the 1880s it was suffering from structural problems and beginning to fail, the foundations of the piers being gradually washed away. The bridge became increasingly fragile, and in 1925 a temporary steel bridge was built next to it in order to take some of the motor traffic, and relieve the pressure on the old bridge.

In the 1930s the decision was taken to demolish Rennie's bridge and replace it with one designed by Sir Giles Gilbert Scott, the architect who designed Battersea Power Station and Britain's iconic red telephone boxes. His new five-span bridge opened in 1942, and remains the version we know today, constructed from reinforced concrete beams clad in Portland stone, held up by adjustable jacks hidden inside the bridge piers, capable of correcting any movement due to further erosion of the foundations.

Waterloo Bridge Station

Designed by William Tite, with Mr Locke as his engineer, the station opened on 11 July 1848, and for the next thirty-five years it was officially known as Waterloo Bridge Station. It was constructed high on a viaduct, or series of arches, over the marshy ground said to have been occupied previously by 'hay stalls, cow yards, dung heaps and other nuisances'. In fact the whole line of the extension from Nine Elms was raised above the boggy ground on a series of arches, and on its way into the station the line was made to twist three times, firstly to avoid Vauxhall Gardens (which existed until 1859), then again to avoid a gas works on the opposite side, and finally to skirt round the gardens of Lambeth Palace.

The station was immediately popular, despite starting with just three platforms and a handful of temporary buildings. It was designed as a through station, the company's intention being to extend even further towards the City at a later date, although this never actually happened. The company directors were therefore reluctant to build any kind of impressive terminus at Waterloo, and although the station was continually expanded during the nineteenth century, all these additions were intended to be temporary. The regular addition of new offices had the effect of creating a poorly laid out station, confusing for those who had to use it. Around 1860, additional platforms were built to the east of the existing ones, increasing the number of platforms to seven and providing yet another new block of offices. This was known as the North Station, and the original set of platforms became known as the Central Station.

For logistical reasons, during the 1860s no trains entered Waterloo Station with their engines. Instead, just outside the station there was a wooden platform where all trains would stop. A man would then attach one end of a rope to the coupling between the engine and the train, and he would stand on the footboard of the first carriage holding the other end of the rope. As the engine pulled the train forwards again, and reaching a speed of about 10mph, the man would pull the coupling open and the engine would run forwards into a siding, while the rest of the train would continue on into the station, stopping by the guard's application of the handbrake. This meant that the engine could be refuelled and attached to the front of the train for the return journey. Doors to the platform were closed five minutes before a train was about to depart, in order to 'prevent undue rush at the last moment'.

Expansion in the Late 1880s

In 1865 plans for a new line from Waterloo Station to Whitehall were revealed, and tunnels were built under the River Thames for this purpose. This was to be the Waterloo and Whitehall Railway, and it was to be a pneumatic railway, powered by air pressure, whereby carriages would be pushed and pulled (or rather blown and sucked) along large enclosed metal tubes. A stationary engine powering the vacuum would be based at Waterloo, and would obviate the need for locomotives and the associated expense. It would also have reduced pollution along the line. Around £70,000 was spent dredging a trench across the Thames into which prefabricated metal tubes were to be placed, supported by brick piers just below the river bed. But the company ran into financial difficulty and in 1871 the whole scheme was dropped.

Above ground, two more platforms were added in 1878, along with new offices and refreshment rooms, and this was officially known as the South Station. However, this being at the height of the British Empire, when events around the world struck pride into the hearts of Britons at home, the South Station soon became known as the 'Cyprus Station', the platforms opening when the island of Cyprus became a British colony following the Cyprus Convention of 4 June 1878.

During the mid-1880s six additional platforms for the Windsor services were built on the northern side of the station. Finished in 1885, the same year that General Gordon died in Khartoum, this area became known as the 'Khartoum Station' and sometimes the 'Abyssinia Station', reflecting political events in that part of the world.

However, each time the station expanded, more people living nearby were evicted, and it is estimated that about 2,000 people lost their homes to make room for these additional extensions to the station.

Each of these mini stations had their own facilities, ticket offices, entrances and platform numbers, which created a confusing experience for passengers. One writer called the station 'a maze without a plan', and jokes were made about trains getting lost amongst the platforms. Indeed, some platform numbers were duplicated, and there was even a railway line that cut right across the passenger concourse, through an archway in the offices, and out to a bridge over the Waterloo Road to the South Eastern Railway's own station, also called Waterloo, but today known as Waterloo East. For many years there was even a platform on the bridge itself located above the road. Today the four platforms at Waterloo East are lettered A to D, rather than numbered, so as to avoid confusion with platforms at the main station.

The Waterloo and City Line

It must be remembered that the ambition of many railway companies was not only to reach London, but also to have a terminus north of the river, where most of the business of the capital took place. On 11 July 1898 HRH the Duke of Cambridge officially opened the Waterloo and City Line, with passenger services starting on 8 August that year. This was one of the earliest underground railways, and the second electric railway in London, and it finally enabled the LSWR to reach the City of London. Basically a shuttle service under the Thames between Waterloo and Bank stations, it quickly became known as 'The Drain'. The rolling stock originally comprised four five-car trains built by Jackson and Sharp, an American company, supported by a couple of carriages build by Dick, Kerr and Company of Preston.

The carriages were of the 'open car' type, with the motor at one end covered by additional seating. This meant that you could choose to sit upstairs or downstairs, on hard wooden seats, since no upholstery was provided in order to keep the carriages clean.

It was an electric system, power being provided by Waterloo's own coal-fired power station. Although to all intents and purposes an underground line, it remained separate from the main London Underground system until 1994, and is still known as the Waterloo and City line, even though the City station has been called Bank since 28 October 1940.

'London Jack'

Back on the main concourse a familiar sight for many passengers would be 'London Jack', a black retriever who spent eight years patrolling the station collecting money for charity. Strapped to his back was a metal collecting tin, and he would bark, shake hands and perform tricks in return for a penny. When he died he was stuffed and put on display in a glass cabinet with a slot for coins at the front. 'From his case at Waterloo station he still appeals to the passengers who pass by', reported the *Sphere* newspaper in 1901. London Jack's son took over the work at Waterloo and was said to stop and look at his late father whenever he passed by. In fact many stations had their own versions of London Jack, and they, too, were often preserved after death in order to carry on their important work.

The Most Badly Organized Station in London

By the end of the nineteenth century around 700 trains per day were arriving and departing at Waterloo. It had become the biggest and most badly organized station in London, but to rebuild it would be a major task. In 1889 the railway economist Sir William Mitchell Acworth wrote:

> It is probable that the Company and the public will both have henceforward to make the best of it. To recast so huge a structure with 100,000 passengers and 700 trains in and out every day of the year is a simple impossibility; a task that unless the population of London all take a holiday for a twelve-month is hardly likely to be so much as attempted.

The station's usage grew because it not only catered for long distance traffic to and from the south coast, but also served vast numbers of daily commuters from the southern Home Counties.

In the evenings the passengers arriving would be pleasure seekers on their way to one of the many theatres close to Waterloo. One such venue was the 'Canterbury', which started life in a public house called the Canterbury Arms or Tavern in 1852. Rebuilt in 1876, and reported to be London's oldest music hall, its entrance was south of the railway tracks leading into the station, while the auditorium was north of them, obliging patrons to walk through a tunnel underneath the entire track layout to reach their seats in the theatre. The tunnel included an aquarium to entertain the visitors as they made their way through. Sadly the building was badly damaged by bombing in 1942, and was finally demolished in 1955.

London Necropolis Station

Near to the entrance to the Canterbury theatre stood the unique and slightly macabre-sounding London Necropolis Station.

Waterloo Necropolis Station, 1892. COPY1/409

London Necropolis Station entrance, 1914. WO32/18165

to avoid upsetting regular passengers. There were two platforms, one for mourners with five separate waiting rooms for the different funeral parties, and the second platform where coffins would be loaded into the trains, completely screened from the view of the mourners. This service ran until severe bomb damage was incurred during World War II, and the station closed on 11 May 1941. The last funeral to be carried on the London Necropolis Railway was that of Edward Irish, a Chelsea pensioner who was buried on 11 April 1941.

In 1911 railway employee Mr Ness Wilson published his reminiscences regarding his work at Waterloo when he started work in the 1870s. He tells one story in which he thought he was about to witness the destruction of the old Guards Room on Platform 5. He had been assisting an older hand to sweep what was then known as the Leatherhead Platform when:

There broke upon the silence of the traf-fic-less station the clanging sound of a most doleful bell. In an instant my companion had thrown aside his broom, and calling on me to follow, had started off at full speed down the platform, shouting 'Fire! Fire!' We found collected round the manual fire-engine all the staff on duty, the fireman himself bustling about attired in a fearful sort of dress – a cross between a diving suit and a beefeater's uniform. We were soon harnessed to the engine, and off at a double quick pace to the scene of the 'conflagra-tion'. In our hurry we actually ran over an old man who had been startled out of his temporary sleeping place (a pile of market baskets on the platform) by the alarm of fire.

Originally located on the east side of Waterloo, and built in 1854, the station relocated in 1902 to the west side of the station at 121 Westminster Bridge Road. The Necropolis Station was entirely devoted to transporting dead bodies, together with their respective mourners from Waterloo, to the fifteen-acre cemetery at Brookwood, near Woking in Surrey – a cemetery set aside for the London dead, since the cemeteries in the capital were now full up and poorly maintained.

Operated by the London Necropolis and National Mausoleum Company, the station was discretely separate from the main station so as

This is the London Necropolis—an imposing *plateau* of five hundred enclosed acres. Here, far away from the din of the unsympathetic crowd, repose in peace many of all ranks who, after "life's fitful fever," have closed their career on earth. Nor, upon observing how a funeral is conducted, can we refrain from endorsing Dr. Sutherland's remarks in his Report to Government on the subject of burial, namely, " that the London Necropolis Company is the only corporation of the kind which combines in its practice a proper regard to public health."

The English Churchman.

London Necropolis at Brookwood Cemetery, 1914.   WO32/18165

'Where is the fire?' I managed to gasp. 'In the Guards' Room,' my neighbour sententiously exclaimed. Arrived outside the Guards' Room we ran out a length of hose, fixed a branch pipe, unscrewed a hydrant, and a dozen men or more commenced pumping for dear life. I could not see either flames or smoke, and began to smell a very large 'rat'. There was a fire, I knew, in the Guards' Room's grate. Could this be the fire we were trying to quench? Alas, so it seemed. All this fuss was only makebelieve – timed by the Night Inspector to see how quickly it could be done, and the performance was technically termed 'wet drill!'

What a lovely example of railway life 140 years ago!

A New Station

With the new Waterloo and City line providing the link to the city that the company had always wanted, it was now obvious that Waterloo would become their permanent London terminus, and in 1899 the decision was taken to demolish the ramshackle station buildings and build a completely new one worthy of representing the LSWR. Groundworks and slum clearance to the south of the station took a couple of years to accomplish, but the first five new platforms to the south were ready in 1909. The builders then gradually worked their way north, creating the new station as they went. World War I hindered construction work for a while, but in 1915 the first electrified service from Waterloo to East Putney was started. Escalators were introduced in 1919, as was the famous four-faced clock, and the new station was finally opened by Queen Mary in 1922.

The main passenger entrance to the station was now the impressive Victory Arch, designed by James Rob Scott, who was to become the Southern Region's chief architect. The baroque design commemorates those 585 employees of the LSWR killed in World War I. Sculpted into the centre of the arch is Britannia holding aloft the torch of Liberty, as she watches over Bellona, the Roman Goddess of War to her right, brandishing a dagger in one hand and a torch of death and destruction in the other. To Britannia's left sits the enthroned figure of Athena signifying courage and wisdom, and offering the branch of a palm tree as a symbol of peace.

Inside the station the 'maze without a plan' had been transformed into the station building we see today. With its twenty-one platforms, 240 clocks, its own telephone exchange and a huge passenger concourse stretching a full 800 feet, the 25-acre station had finally become a terminus of which the LSWR could enjoy a short-lived pride. Short-lived because the following year the company would no longer exist, being subsumed into the new Southern Railway at the grouping in 1923, along with the London Brighton and South Coast Railway, and the South Eastern and Chatham Railway.

Waterloo Station became the headquarters of the Southern Railway under Sir Herbert Walker KCB. He had been general manager of

A glimpse of the redeveloped Waterloo Station, 1910. ZSPC11/560

WEH-LYN
RAILWAY RECORDS

HOLLAND BROWNE

THE HUB OF A BUSY RAILWAY. ZSPC 11/s'60 53
A glimpse of the new Waterloo terminus of the London and South Western Railway.

19

the LSWR, and was a gifted man who successfully brought the three rival companies together at the grouping. Tall and impressive, he was respected and revered by all who worked with him. On 27 May 1952 a memorial plaque to him was unveiled with a bronze cameo portrait set in the stonework just inside the York Road entrance to Waterloo Station. It commemorates his thirty-six years of work for the LSWR and the SR, during which he oversaw the rebuilding of the station and the complete electrification of the Southern Railway. He was a man of determination, foresight, patience and modesty. His criticism could be severe if deserved, though he did not bear grudges, and his praise was short but genuine – it meant a lot to those who heard him say 'Thank you, old man – that will do.'

In the 1930s there were further improvements to the station, including loudspeakers in 1932, a News Reel cinema next to platform 1 in 1934, and a compete overhaul of the signalling system during the night of 16 May 1936, when 1,000 men worked together to change the station over from the old semaphore system to new electric light signalling with automatic points.

Station Life

Like any railway station, all of human life is represented by those passing through, and by those who earn their living at these great meeting places. Not everyone is doing so legally, however, as in the case of Martin Joseph Sweeney, who was arrested in November 1951 for stealing a suitcase from platform 19. This was after he had enjoyed three double brandies and a packet of Players cigarettes at the 227 Bar, before admitting he had no money with which to pay for them. When questioned by the police he stated his name was 'Sweeney Todd, but without the razor'. He was sentenced to six months' imprisonment at Tower Bridge Magistrates Court, and the Restaurant Car & Refreshment Department at Waterloo sought legal advice on whether licensed premises must accept money before serving drinks.

And then there is the case of Albert Edward Pearce, who was arrested for being a reputed thief loitering at Waterloo Station on 11 January 1940 with intent to steal luggage. Pearce was seen attempting to take a large pigskin suitcase belonging to a couple while they examined the departure board. Luckily the couple turned round just as he was reaching for the bag, and he walked briskly away towards the booking hall. Here he tried again to take an unattended bag: he was about to snatch a large leather suitcase when a woman came from the ticket office, picked up the bag and walked away.

Pearce continued to prowl around the buffet looking at more bags, when he noticed that Detective Sergeant Crawford of the Metropolitan Police was watching him. He quickly walked to the front booking office, bought a ticket and ran to platform 2, where he was arrested. He gave a false name, but Pearce was known to the police: had been convicted five times before, twice in Australia, for various offences dating back to 1920.

At his trial he was sentenced to three months' hard labour at the Tower Bridge Police Court on 26 January 1940, but he appealed against this sentence on the grounds that he could not be a 'reputed thief' owing to the length of time since his last conviction. He was released on bail, and promptly re-arrested for attempted pickpocketing on 14 February 1940. Again released on bail, surety for his release was in the form of

£50 provided by John Silvester Maynard, alias Silvio Luigi Mazzardi, referred to by the police as an Italian 'assassin' who was a continual associate of thieves and a suspected receiver of stolen goods. Maynard was constantly standing surety for criminals, and basically ran an organized crime ring, like Fagin overseeing Pearce's role as the (not so) Artful Dodger.

Delays in the prosecution process indicate that Pearce managed to avoid his prison sentence. The troublesome Maynard, however, was removed from the scene when he was arrested and detained under Section 18B of the Defence Regulations, 1939, which allowed for the internment of people suspected of being Nazi sympathizers. Some creative police work meant that the Italian criminal mastermind was, as it says in the case file, 'satisfactorily dealt with.'

The Station under Attack in World War II

During World War II the arches upon which the station was built were used as air-raid shelters, and became home to 500 people who had been bombed out. In May 1941 Waterloo was badly damaged by German Luftwaffe bombing, and the station was completely closed for a week while repairs were made to enable half the services to run again; it took a month before all the services were back to normal.

The station came under attack again on the night of 31 October 1945, but this time from Major the Hon. John Bingham, son of George Charles Bingham, 5th Earl of Lucan, and Uncle of Richard John Bingham, 7th Earl of Lucan – the same Lord Lucan who was to disappear in 1974 after murdering his nanny. However, it wasn't his nephew disappearing that was the issue, but the station master at Waterloo. Bingham had been in foggy London with his wife and had arrived at the station at 10.15pm to find a queue of about a hundred people waiting for the Ascot train. There was no information on the indicator board as to the platform from which the Ascot train would leave, or when it was due to leave, since departure was delayed by the fog. The buffet was closed, there were no announcements, and the station master's office was deserted.

His train finally left at midnight, and the following day Bingham wrote a blistering letter to the Passenger Traffic Manager of the Southern Railway suggesting that it was the duty of the company to advertise the times of trains and to keep the public informed. He said that the buffet should remain open as long as trains were arriving or departing, that an official should be available at all times in the station master's office, and that the loudspeaker system should be used as long as traffic is using the station. He appreciated that war-time handicaps still existed, but it was time that efforts should be made to stop regarding the public as 'docile and infinitely patient cattle.'

Then, using a colourful turn of phrase, he added that the sight of that many people waiting needlessly reminded him of crowds in Indian stations, 'but whereas in the Orient inefficiency is normally ascribed to the Will of Allah, in England we consider ourselves entitled to demand that a Public Service such as a railway company should regard the convenience of the public as a paramount duty'.

Mr Smart, Superintendent of Operations, obsequiously replied to Bingham expressing regret for the inconvenience suffered, and assuring him that the several matters to which he had kindly drawn attention would receive attention. However, Sir Eustace Missenden, General Manager of the Southern Railway, wrote to the Railway Executive Committee demolishing each point highlighted by Bingham in his letter, and stating that 'Major the Hon. John Bingham evidently does not appreciate the reactionary effect such delays [due to fog] can cause.'

In the spring of 1942 during the dark days of World War II when air-raid precautions meant that no lights could be used as they might attract German aircraft, experimental equipment was installed by the Southern Railway at Waterloo Station, to discover whether fluorescent markings would help in the movement of passengers during blackout hours. The experiments were carried out for the Ministry of Home Security: it was thought that fluorescent paint energized by ultra-violet light might help people find their way at particular points such as staircases and road crossings, without contravening the Lighting (Restrictions) Order, 1940.

Fluorescent markings were applied to the handrails at the memorial arch entrance stairway, the stairs to the Bakerloo line at platform 21, and the road crossing between the main station and Waterloo East, and a luminous 'Telephones' sign was installed by a cab exit. Each of these was lit by tungsten lamps with black-glass filters, or mercury lamps to provide the ultra-violet light.

The conclusions reached by Southern Railway were that the use of fluorescent paint was in most cases worse than authorized category 'B' illumination, that black-bulb mercury lamps were better than filtered tungsten lamps, and that a lamp that was too close to the paint might well contravene lighting restrictions, while another that was slightly further away was ineffective. No further experiments appear to have been conducted.

Advertising in Railway Stations

Railway stations are the ideal location for advertising. With thousands of people passing through each day an advertising pitch can be a lucrative money spinner, and in 1975 John Nunneley, Managing Director of British Transport Advertising Ltd, came up with a unique idea to make the most of the available space at Waterloo, to guarantee £7,000 per year in rental, to enhance the station free of charge, and to bring an international flavour to British Rail at a time when Britain had just joined the European Economic Community. His idea was to arrange for a large mural to be erected in front of the old News Cinema near platform 1, which would combine art, publicity and industry. He contacted Olivetti, the typewriter and electronics company, who then commissioned the renowned Belgian surrealist artist Jean-Michel Folon to create a bespoke advertisement in the form of a huge painting.

The mural was painted on canvas sixty-eight feet long and twenty-eight feet high, it weighed six tons, and featured a striking landscape of sand dunes amongst which little men in blue coats strolled about. From behind the dunes several words stood like skyscrapers, including 'Travel', 'Hello', 'Tomorrow', 'Data processing', and of course, 'Olivetti'. Folon named the artwork 'Paysage', which translates as 'Landscape' in English, and this was his most important work so far in the UK, although he had recently completed a large painting for the Brussels Underground, and was also exhibiting in Japan.

The painting was unveiled by Richard Marsh, Chairman of British Rail, on 12 May 1975, in front of an invited audience of 500 VIP guests, many of them businessmen. In his speech Marsh made the most of the fact that it was an Italian company that had invited a Belgian artist to create a piece for a British railway station – it was indeed a Common Market occasion. The new installation bridged the gap between art and advertising, it informed travellers, making their journeys more agreeable, and contributed to BR revenues. More than 200,000 people per day would pass through Waterloo, which was more than would see the painting in a month if it were displayed at the National Gallery.

However, not everyone was happy about the new artwork, or the way in which it had been commissioned. Some members of the Public Relations and Publicity Department of the British Railways Board resented the way that British Transport Advertising Limited had forced their plans into effect, in what might have been regarded as their territory. One employee felt that the unveiling of the largest canvas artwork in Europe, which dominated the station concourse, was merely 'a gimmick to persuade several hundred business executives to attend a function to promote Olivetti's electronics', while the Controller of the Public Relations and Publicity Department, Eric Merrill, stated that the best thing about the mural would be the annual income, adding: 'From the far end of the station, I concede, it adds a splash of colour.'

Awkward letters had passed between the two departments in the run-up to the launch, and the final spat between them was in August of that year, when John Nunneley wrote to Merrill, rather belatedly, asking him to contribute to the costs of a short film he had commissioned showing the opening ceremony. Merrill wrote a single sentence back stating that he had not undertaken to bear the cost of this film, nor was he prepared to do so. Nunneley replied: 'I have looked again at my letter to you dated 12 August to see whether it so lacked in courtesy as to call forth from you your curt note in reply. I am satisfied that no courtesy was lacking on my own part.'

'Waterloo International'

From 1994 to 2007 the five western-most platforms at Waterloo were dedicated to the Eurostar international train service to France and Belgium. They were managed separately from the main station and branded as 'Waterloo International'. Four of these platforms were built specially for this service, which was timed to begin in conjunction with the opening of the Channel Tunnel.

The tunnel was opened by the Queen on 6 May 1994 in a joint ceremony with the French President François Mitterand, and the first Eurostar train to leave Waterloo left on 14 November 1994. However, Eurostar trains had to use the existing busy and winding tracks from Waterloo, and when the UK's first high-speed main line was built through Kent and opened in 1998, the Eurostar service had to relocate to St Pancras. The last train to leave Waterloo for the continent left on 13 November 2007, exactly thirteen years to the day after the very first one. The following day Eurostar trains left London from their new base at St Pancras Station. During their time at Waterloo, Eurostar had carried almost eighty-two million passengers to and from the continent.

Waterloo Station Today

Today over ninety-nine million people enter and leave Waterloo Station each year. It has twenty-three escalators, twenty-four platforms, and 130 automated ticket gates from the concourse, and another twenty-seven in the subway below. The five ex-Eurostar platforms are due to reopen by the end of 2018, and other platforms will be lengthened to accommodate even longer trains, as the life and development of Britain's busiest railway station continues to evolve. ⚙

Waterloo signal box. COPY1409/219

Collision between an empty train and a passenger train, Waterloo 1960. MT114/299

Chapter 5

KING'S CROSS, 1852

THE NAME 'KING'S CROSS' REFERS TO an area of London near Camden and Islington, as well as to the railway station of that name. The name came about owing to the junction, or cross-roads, where four major roads meet: the New Road (now the Euston Road), the Gray's Inn Road, the Caledonian Road and the Pentonville Road. It was at this location that a new and striking monument to King George IV, who had passed away on 26 June 1830, was erected later that same year, and the site became known as the King's Crossroads. The monument was sixty feet high, and included an eleven-foot statue of the King, standing upon a small octagonal building, which included a clock. It was paid for by public subscription and was supposed to be an impressive memorial to the King, but he had been extremely unpopular due to his drunkenness and his lavish life-style, and not enough money was raised for the monument.

The four statues that were to be placed at each corner never materialized, and despite the building being completed in 1830, it wasn't until 1835 that the statue of the King was placed on top. The effigy was poorly made, and cost a mere £25 to create. It was built from bricks and mortar, and painted to look like stone. Far from being a fine example of Georgian architecture, it was actually rather a shoddy embarrassment. The writer George Walter Thornbury said at the time that it was a 'ridiculous octagonal structure crowned by an absurd statue', and the figure was removed in 1842.

The rest of the building remained for three more years before changing use to become first a police station and then a pub. It was finally demolished in 1845 as it had become a hazard to traffic. However, the short-lived inferior statue gave rise to the title 'King's Cross', which has remained the name of this inner city area of London for the last 180 years.

King's Cross Station was built at a cost of £123,000, as the London terminus of the Great Northern Railway (GNR), and opened on 14 October 1852. The previous temporary terminus had been at Maiden Lane since 1850, a short distance to the north of King's Cross, and now known as York Way. The new station was built on a ten-acre site close to an area originally occupied since 1802 by a fever hospital, and a smallpox hospital, which had been there since 1767. The smallpox hospital provided free inoculations for the poor, the only London hospital to do so at that time. The GNR spent £65,000 on purchasing the land and demolishing the hospitals.

Archaeological excavations appear to show that the Romans used to cross through the Fleet River at this point, and it became known as Broad Ford, a 'ford' being a shallow part of a stream

King's Cross Station, from a photograph taken between 1878 and 1883. RAIL236/627

suitable for crossing. It was near here that, in AD61, the Queen of the Iceni tribe, Boudicca, was killed in a battle with the Roman invaders. Later on, when a bridge was built over the ford, it became known as 'Battle Bridge'. The spot is located in the space that now exists between King's Cross and St Pancras stations, and it is said that the body of Boudicca is buried beneath one of the platforms at King's Cross Station.

King's Cross Station Design

King's Cross Station was designed by Lewis Cubitt, the civil engineer who had previously built London Bridge Station and a number of bridges in the British colonies around the world. His intention was to build King's Cross as a bold and impressive station, but not to waste time and money on unnecessary flourishes. He wanted to design a functional building; its usefulness would be derived from its simple layout based on practicality and space. He deliberately avoided creating an embellished advertisement for the railway company – which ironically is exactly what was built next door fifteen years later, when

the ornate and elaborate St Pancras Station was built by the rival Midland Railway Company.

The main features of the new station were a heavy-looking frontage with twin arched windows and a central clock tower. Cubitt allowed himself one superfluous indulgence in giving the 112-foot clock tower an Italianate roof, three internal bells (bass, tenor and treble) and a weather vane. The clock itself had been made by E. J. Dent, the expert clock and watchmaker, for the Great Exhibition in Hyde Park, but after the exhibition was over, the clock needed a permanent home. On 4 August 1851 Dent wrote to Mr Denison, chairman of the GNR, saying that he would be proud to have the clock 'in your tower'. The clock had gained credit not only for its construction but also for its performance, not having lost a second in six weeks while at the Great Exhibition, and he was happy to let it go for £200. The company accepted the offer, and the clock was installed with three illuminated faces, the face on the north side of the tower overlooking the engine shed roof being left blank.

The clock was adapted to enable the quarter hours to be struck. The dials were installed ninety feet from the ground, and each dial was nine feet in diameter. Denison thought that the tower would need to be redesigned to include windows above the clock to enable the sound of the bells to be heard, and to let in enough light for attendants to see the mechanism, but this was found to be unnecessary. Dent had an excellent reputation, having previously built the Royal Exchange clock, which was installed in 1844, and he went on to win the contract to supply the great clock for the Palace of Westminster in 1852, erroneously known as Big Ben. Unfortunately he died before this was finished, but his adopted son completed the work. The King's Cross clock struck the hour and the quarters from 1852, although striking stopped in 1914 at the outbreak of World War I and was not resumed until 1924. Striking was again halted three years later, and the bells were melted down after World War II. Perhaps the strangest quality of the King's Cross clock was that its hands moved in half seconds instead of seconds.

The rest of the station was built in plain yellow London brick with virtually no decoration. Behind the frontage, and following the lines of the arched windows, were two huge semi-circular roofs, 800 feet long. Unusually, the ribs holding the glass roof lights in place were not iron but constructed from timber planks screwed together and held in place by iron supports. These wooden 'beams' were light and cheap, and gave Cubitt more flexibility in his design – but by the late 1860s problems with the roof led to the wooden sections of the eastern train shed having to be replaced by metal structures. Lack of ventilation meant that the wooden beams had become rotten, and the western roof also required similar refurbishment in 1886 at a cost of £18,500, the work being undertaken by Andrew Handyside and Company of the Britannia Ironworks, Derby.

Cubitt gave King's Cross one arrival platform and one departure platform, with fourteen siding tracks in between, which were originally used for storage. Despite being the largest station in Britain when built, it quickly proved inadequate in dealing with high passenger numbers, particularly since the GNR allowed Midland trains to use the station before they had their own London terminus. Custom was generated not only through long distance routes from Edinburgh, Aberdeen and the northern shires of England, but also from commuters travelling

W. Prisley's 'day and night' advertising rail lamp.   RAIL1057/3147

into London from the Home Counties via branch lines added during the 1850s and 1860s. A dedicated suburban station was added on the west side of the main building, but the GNR found it impossible to keep up with the increasing passenger numbers. Additional platforms were added in 1893 and 1895 to help the station cope with the increased passenger traffic.

Lamps and Weighing Machines

Any large commercial innovation will attract smaller companies, which will try to make money in a symbiotic relationship with the larger company. One such concern was Prisley and Co., based at No. 9 Pancras Lane, in the City, which manufactured translucent advertisements which could be attached to existing gas lamps. They also made complete pendant or pedestal lamps adorned with advertisements. Prisley approached the GNR repeatedly in 1860 regarding their patented 'Day and Night Advertising Lamps', which they offered to install at King's Cross, in complete agreement with their engineer, for which they would pay the railway company £1 per annum per lamp. Records show that the GNR were sympathetic to the idea, although they already had a contract with Messrs Smith & Son of 186 Strand, who were unhappy about the prospect, and felt that the move would be contrary to the spirit of their agreement.

A similar proposal was submitted to the GNR in April 1871 from a Mr Read of 56 Acton Street, Gray's Inn Road, who wished to install two weighing machines for use by the general public at King's Cross. The charge to the weight-conscious traveller would be 1d, and the correct weight reading was apparently guaranteed. Mr Read would pay the GNR £50 per annum to install such a machine, which he would pay quarterly. The application was forwarded to the GNR directors, and in his covering letter the General Manager at King's Cross writes that:

> ...machines of this sort may be seen standing on the Metropolitan platforms, and passengers are accosted by the boy keepers with the somewhat familiar cry of 'Try your weight, Gentlemen!' I hardly imagine you will approve these machines being admitted to your platforms, but as

the rent of £50 a year for two of them seems rather a high bid, I beg leave to submit it for your consideration.

The directors accepted the proposal, with the proviso that the GNR were to maintain 'some control over Mr Read's assistants'.

GNR Funeral Service

Many people will have heard of the Necropolis Station at Waterloo, but King's Cross also had a similar arrangement dating from 1855, when the Great Northern London Cemetery Company established a burial ground at Colney Hatch, now known as New Southgate, about seven miles from King's Cross. The cemetery comprised around 150 acres, and the company entered into an agreement with the GNR to run a funeral service there. They allowed the GNR to build a railway station next to the burial ground on their land, and the GNR built another on their own land at Maiden Lane just outside King's Cross. The Maiden Lane building was part mortuary and part railway station, with stained-glass windows and a wedge-shaped, steeple-like tower at one end.

The GNR aimed to provide a cheaper funeral service to families who could not afford the cost of the Waterloo Necropolis services, with the added benefit that the dead body could be stored hygienically at the station until the funeral, instead of being left at home. This was before refrigeration, and so gas jets were used to maintain a continual flow of air from the mortuary, to help preserve the body until burial.

Coffins arriving at the station would be lowered by mechanical lift on to rails, where they would be transported to a vault at platform level for temporary storage. Mourners could access the mortuary at any time to pay their respects, and at first a daily train would convey the dead, together with mourners, the short journey to the cemetery. However, usage was not as high as expected, and the frequency of trains was gradually reduced to one per week. The cost was 6s per coffin, plus 1s 6d per mourner.

It was a cheap and convenient service, running from 1861, but the amount of traffic between the two stations did not justify maintaining the line, and by 1873 the funeral service had ceased to

Roof over the platform at King's Cross in 1869. RAIL236/625

Another view of the front of King's Cross, dating from 1878–1883. RAIL236/626

operate. The station building at New Southgate survived until *c.*1904 before being demolished, while the Maiden Lane mortuary fell into disrepair and was finally pulled down in the 1960s. It seems that the cemetery, being so close to London, meant that there was little benefit in using the service over that provided by the more traditional horse-drawn hearse.

Problems with Cab Drivers

In October 1867 a petition was received by the GNR, signed by eighty men employed as Great Northern Railway Privilege Cab Drivers, requesting a place of shelter and refuge, for use by the men while awaiting the arrival of trains. A further petition was submitted in October 1869, adding that the nature of their employment in all weathers meant that they could not be blamed for giving in to the 'temptation of a good fire at the nearest tap room'. However, having their own rest room at the station would help them to avoid intemperance, their wives and families would be better cared for, and 'they would hold in happy remembrance, and give you lasting gratitude for the boon'.

Their petition explained that they were absent from their families for about seventeen hours each day, and they often had to wait up to four hours for a train and the possibility of a fare, with nowhere to wait other than a public house. Between them they carried upwards of 30,000 passengers per year, and each man would be happy to pay 2d per week for a warm room at the station in which to wait.

A year later a third petition signed by ninety-four cab drivers was submitted to the GNR Board on 4 October 1870, but by this time the Board had already identified a suitable room at the top of a stone staircase, which would cost £150 to prepare (as long as they used old materials) and £22 per year for heating and lighting. With 100 cab drivers each paying 2d per week, the Board estimated that the income would amount to £44 per year, and the initial outlay would be repaid in about fourteen years' time. So the cold, damp and tipsy cab drivers, having waited three years, finally got their waiting room.

In May 1883 the rival South Eastern Railway Company carried out an experiment at their stations with a new 'open-station' cab system, whereby any cab was allowed to collect passengers from their stations for 1d each time they entered the station. This was a departure from the old system where certain 'privilege cabs' paid 3s 6d per week to collect fares. Henry Oakley, chief clerk in the General Manager's Office at King's Cross, was interested in the scheme and wondered whether it could be adopted by the GNR at King's Cross. He consulted with SER officials regarding the new scheme, but was told that receipts at Charing Cross had actually fallen by £200 over four months, that the cabmen and horses were of a much lower class than previously, and that passenger complaints had been numerous. There had even been seven cases of obstruction and assault by cabmen.

London Bridge and Cannon Street stations had also lost money under the new system, and passengers had complained about the conduct of the new cabmen, who disregarded orders, and used cabs and horses that were decidedly inferior. The scheme was damaging the reputation of the SER.

In January 1884 the secretary of the Amalgamated Cab Drivers' Society wrote to the GNR acknowledging that the experiment has not been a success, but seeking permission to set up their own payment collection office at King's Cross, which would collect the cab admission revenue at 1d per entry, and have the power to refuse entry to substandard cabs. The GNR Board was not convinced. They did not wish to risk upsetting their customers with inferior cabs and awkward cabmen, and they chose to remain with their existing privilege cab system. Moreover, they undertook to inspect cabs more frequently,

and even decided to examine the possibility of acquiring a number of brand new, high class cabs known as 'Forder's Hansoms' from Forder and Co., carriage makers to the Prince of Wales.

Station Problems in the Late 1880s

As traffic through King's Cross Station increased, the Board sought new ways to ease congestion. One significant problem suffered by the station was the approach tunnel a short distance to the north near some gas works, which took the line under Regent's Canal. This was called Gasworks Tunnel, and was in effect a bottleneck, as all trains had to pass through here before reaching the station. Initially there were only two lines through the tunnel, one up and one down track. However, in 1878 and 1892 two more tunnels were built, each with two lines, which significantly improved congestion.

Another problem with the station was that the glass roof acted like a greenhouse, and on

Euston Road, 1899. COPY1/442

King's Cross goods station in 1911, where goods could be unloaded on to the Regent's Canal. ZLIB3/19

King's Cross Goods Station, connected with Regent's Canal
27

New goods station interior at King's Cross, 1911. ZLIB3/19

NEW GOODS SHED AT KING'S CROSS (G.N.R.), INTERIOR.

sunny days the temperature inside the station would become unbearable. In June 1854 Lewis Cubitt came up with a novel idea to help keep the temperature down. He suggested spraying the glass roofing panels with fresh cold water from the nearby canal, pumped up to a system of perforated pipes laid out along the centre of each of the two roof structures. The cooling water would then trickle down on to the lower panes of glass, over the slating and into the gutters. The station master would control the flow of water using a lever outside his office, and Lewis submitted a plan with red-coloured copper tubes and little blue jets marked where the water would pass through the perforations.

After much consideration, however, Lewis Cubitt's colleague Joseph Cubitt (no relation), the civil engineer who practically built the whole of the Great Northern Railway, was not convinced this idea would work. He wrote to the directors on 29 June 1854 admitting that there was no actual data to work from, but to make any difference to the temperature of the glass there would need to be a flow of 7,000 gallons of water per hour over the entire roof, adding up to 42,000 gallons on days when the sun might shine for six hours continuously. To install pipes capable of delivering this amount of water would cost £1,020, and while the system would no doubt cool the glass panels of the roof, he courteously pointed out that the temperature inside the station was caused by the sun's rays which passed through the glass, and he doubted that the temperature of the glass itself would very much affect the power of the sun's rays. The idea was dropped, and in this snapshot of the thought processes of two great engineers it seems that physics won the argument over design.

The Great Northern Hotel

Opening in 1854, the Great Northern Hotel was built a few yards to the west of the actual station. Like the station itself, the hotel was designed by Lewis Cubitt and was built in a comparatively plain style, with just a hint of Italianate flair. Six storeys high, the line of the building followed the curve of the old Pancras Road, giving it a unique and stately curvature, which today is even more noticeable since the road layout has changed and its demure arc, now apparently included for art's sake alone, echoes the Georgian town houses of Bath. With high ceilings and large windows overlooking a planted flower garden cultivated between it and the station, the little hotel was a gem worthy of the company.

Proposed Improvements to the Station Frontage

Within a few years of King's Cross opening, the plain but grand frontage designed by Cubitt began to be obscured by a collection of random ramshackle buildings thrown up on the forecourt. These included a full sized show-house put up by a building company to promote the London suburbs, and various newspaper stands and shops, the whole effect being one of a shabby shanty town – indeed, the area was sometimes referred to as the 'African Village'. This was made worse in the early 1930s when ten new lock-up shops were built on the site, owned by the LNER and leased out to a variety of businesses including a caterer, a tailor, a sweetshop, a florist and fruiterer, a stationer's, and a dealer in radio and electrical accessories and bicycles.

During 1888 and 1889 extensive plans were drawn up to sweep away the shanty town and to build offices and shops, up to three storeys high, on the land in front of the station. This was land owned by the GNR, and some of the offices were to be occupied by GNR departments, while other offices and shops were to be leased out at a profit to other companies. Fourteen building contractors submitted tenders for the work, and S. W. Pattinson of Ruskington, Sleaford, Lincolnshire were given the contract to erect the new building.

Preliminary work began, but the GNR had not considered the fact that the tunnels of the Metropolitan Railway ran directly under the site. A hastily written letter from the Engineer's Department of the Metropolitan Railway in January 1889 pointed out that the weight of the new building might well cause the tunnels, and therefore the new building, to collapse. The Metropolitan suggested using an inverted arch structure to support the weight of the construction, but both companies thought that the other company should pay for it, and everyone agreed that it was going to be very expensive and complicated to install. The situation was made worse by the realization that the Metropolitan Railway had not paid the GNR any money for building tunnels through GNR-owned land, and the result was a stalemate.

The idea was shelved, and no such large-scale offices or shops were built on the land at that time, and the 'African Village' persisted right through until 1972 when British Rail finally replaced the buildings with a 'Southern Concourse'. This served to tidy up the frontage to the station, but was in itself a sprawling, bland-looking, covered concourse extension housing a ticket office, shops and a waiting area. It was functional, but still had the effect of masking Cubitt's original station façade.

Long-Distance Services to Scotland

At the grouping in 1923 the Great Northern Railway was subsumed into the London and North Eastern Railway (LNER), and the station's long-distance services to Scotland and the north of England appeared to take priority over commuter services. The most famous of these was the *Flying Scotsman*, a 400-mile service to Edinburgh, which departed King's Cross each day at 10am, pulled by one of Sir Nigel Gresley's iconic Pacific locomotives. This service began on 1 May 1928 and became the headline run, although there were other equally impressive services to Newcastle, known as the *Silver Jubilee*, introduced in 1935, and a 6½ hour non-stop express service to Edinburgh known as the *Elizabethan Express*, which began in 1953 and continued into the mid-1960s.

On 3 July 1938 the famous Class A4 locomotive *Mallard* arrived in King's Cross Station following its record-breaking run down the East Coast Main Line, where it reached the speed of 126mph between Little Bytham and Essendine. This was the fastest speed ever reached by a steam engine, a record that still stands today. The driver was sixty-one-year-old Joseph Duddington, who later said that he could have reached 130mph if he had not had to slow down for the junctions at Essendine.

World War II Damage

During World War II the roof of King's Cross Station was damaged by German bombing, and in 1945 an LNER committee was set up to decide whether Cubitt's impressive roof should be repaired, or replaced. The existing roof had 'grave disadvantages' in that constant repainting of the ironwork and cleaning of the glass was costing £3,500 per year. Smoke from the trains meant that maximum daylight was never achieved, and additional lighting was a necessity even at mid-day, adding to overall costs. There was much discussion as to the cost of replacing the roof with an umbrella-style concrete flat roof, which was seen as more practical and would allow smoke to disperse more freely, although its planned open design was liable to subject passengers to wind and rain. This roof, however, would cost in the region of £340,000, whereas to repair the section damaged by the Luftwaffe would cost a mere £21,000.

Thankfully the original design was saved after one of the directors, Mr Fitzherbert-Wright, pointed out that they should spend as little as possible in view of future expenditure requirements on things such as electrification. With a government contribution the cost to the company could be as little as £10,000, he added. The hole in the roof was therefore repaired in May 1946, the work being carried out by Samuel Butler and Company Ltd, of Leeds, and Cubitt's arches were saved.

View from the British Telecom Tower on to King's Cross and St Pancras stations, 1961–1967. CM22/195

Improvements in the Late 1900s

During the 1970s and 1980s the whole King's Cross area was known for being shabby, run-down, neglected and seedy. Its reputation was not helped when a terrible fire broke out on the Piccadilly Line underneath King's Cross on 18 November 1987, killing thirty-one and injuring another 100 people. The fire started on a wooden escalator, probably when a smoker dropped a match, having lit their cigarette on their way out of the station. The grease on the running track of the escalator then caught fire,

and within minutes the wooden escalator was aflame. Hot gases from the fire gathered at the top of the escalator shaft, heating the many layers of ancient paint lining the ceiling, until the heat could be contained no longer – fifteen minutes after the fire started a huge sheet of flame in the form of a flashover shot out of the escalator shaft, filling the ticket hall, and killing most of the people therein.

The fire led to a number of changes in railway and underground practices and regulations across the network, including the replacement of wooden escalators, new fire regulations, the

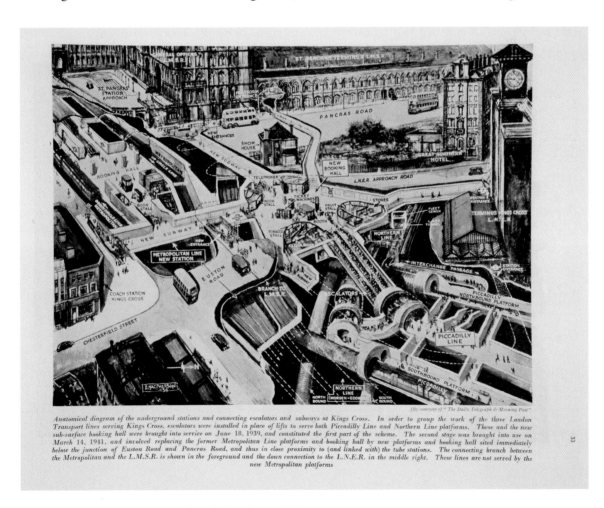

Anatomical diagram of the underground stations and connecting escalators and subways at Kings Cross. In order to group the work of the three London Transport lines serving Kings Cross, escalators were installed in place of lifts to serve both Piccadilly Line and Northern Line platforms. These and the new sub-surface booking hall were brought into service on June 18, 1939, and constituted the first part of the scheme. The second stage was brought into use on March 14, 1941, and involved replacing the former Metropolitan Line platforms and booking hall by new platforms and booking hall sited immediately below the junction of Euston Road and Pancras Road, and thus in close proximity to (and linked with) the tube stations. The connecting branch between the Metropolitan and the L.M.S.R. is shown in the foreground and the down connection to the L.N.E.R. in the middle right. These lines are not served by the new Metropolitan platforms

King's Cross underground schematic, by Douglas Macpherson, 1939. ZLIB8/92 introduction of heat detectors and sprinkler systems, and better telecommunication equipment for station staff.

Improvements in the New Millennium

The main difficulty with King's Cross Station was always that it was too small. The platforms came right up close to the station façade leaving very little room for waiting areas, offices, shops, ticket sales or luggage facilities, and with the station being a listed building, very little restructuring could be undertaken. The tunnels just outside the station meant that the platforms could not be extended in any way as there was no room to do so before the tracks converged. The solution was to go sideways – to build a new modern concourse to the west of the station, in the gap leading up to the hotel. This would have the benefit of bringing together the western suburban train platforms, the main station, the hotel, and access to the underground, and it would allow for the clearance of the Southern Concourse, opening up the station frontage. Thus the idea for an ultra-modern passenger concourse was born.

Before this could be done the main station underwent refurbishment in 2009: thirty-two layers of paint were stripped from the wrought-iron roof structure, which was then repainted a blue-grey colour, with new Welsh slate being used along the lower sides of the roof. Five overlapping layers of glass panels went in along the top of the roof, replacing the old corrugated plastic sheets and roofing felt. The tide began to turn for King's Cross, and things began to improve for the old station.

The new Western Concourse came into use in 2012 at a cost of £180 million. It was built in a semi-circle, reflecting the curve of the Great Northern Hotel, and is unashamedly modern. The roof is constructed from a combination of glass triangles and aluminium supports. It rises to nineteen metres in height, and from within the sixteen main columns can be seen rising up and spreading out across the roof in a tree-like spider's web, abutting the side of the original building. Despite its modern design, the new addition serves only to complement Cubitt's original building. There is no doubt as to which parts are original and which are new, but the overall effect is one of a mutual respect between the two designs.

In 2013 the tired and uninspiring Southern Concourse was finally demolished, and the 'new' King's Cross Square was born – a 7,000 square metre paved open space designed by architect Stanton Williams, where the public can now meet and relax on seating, with ornamental trees and space to move. For the first time in 140 years, visitors can at last admire the iconic Victorian frontage of King's Cross Station unencumbered, as Cubitt designed it to be. As all passengers now leave the station on to the new King's Cross Square with the heavy functional station wall behind them, the theatrically palatial St Pancras to the right, and the historic Euston Station a few yards down the road, there must be little doubt in their minds that they have reached the railway capital of the world. ✿

PADDINGTON, 1854

MUCH OF PADDINGTON STATION AS we know it today was the work of the great engineer Isambard Kingdom Brunel, who designed the station to be the Great Western Railway's grand and impressive London terminus.

A Railway Line from Bristol to London

The story behind Paddington Station began in 1832 when a committee of four Bristol-based businessmen met to discuss building a railway line from Bristol to London. The men were Thomas Guppy, John Harford, George Jones and William Tothill. Guppy was a civil engineer, and became a good friend and business partner with Brunel, working with him on designs for ships as well as railways. John Harford was a wealthy banker and merchant, while Tothill had trained as a surgeon but did not practise, and owned a chemical factory in Bristol. Brunel was informed of their plans in the February of that year, and that they were receiving applications for the post of engineer: the successful applicant would be whoever could supply the line for the cheapest cost. Brunel wrote to the committee stating that his submission would not be the cheapest, but it would be the best.

Brunel discovered that he had been appointed as engineer to the Bristol Railway Company on

Isambard Kingdom Brunel. RAIL1014/21

6 March 1833, and that he was to undertake his survey of the route to London with the Bristol Railway's own engineer William Townsend. Townsend was a local man with limited experience compared to Brunel, who found him frustrating to work alongside. Brunel wrote in his diary 'how the devil I am to get on with him tied to my neck I know not'. Nevertheless, the survey was completed and the results published

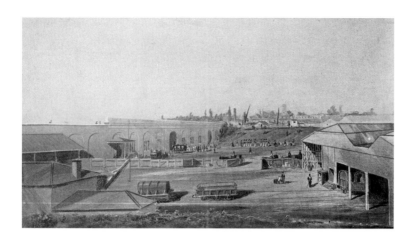

on 30 July 1833. On 27 August Brunel's post was confirmed as engineer to the Bristol Railway, which changed its name to the Great Western Railway (GWR) on the same day.

Raising enough money for the line proved problematic, and the company were forced to submit their Bill to Parliament in October covering only the two end sections of the line, from London to Reading, and from Bristol to Bath. They planned to submit a further Bill covering the middle section of the line when the rest of the money was raised. After much discussion over several months, the House of Lords finally rejected the Bill in July 1834.

One of the main objections was the intention to build the London terminus at Vauxhall, so the company amended their proposal to include a terminus at Euston, which they would share with the London and Birmingham Railway. A year later, on 31 August 1835, the GWR's second parliamentary bill received royal assent, and at a meeting of GWR directors on 15 September 1835 Brunel was confirmed as engineer-in-chief to the company on a handsome salary of £2,000 per annum, with £300 in lieu of travel expenses, and permission to appoint three other engineers of his choice.

Brunel was insistent that the new railway should be built as a 7ft-gauge railway, and he persuaded the company directors that this would be the right thing to do. He had noticed that the carriages on George Stephenson's narrower 4ft 8½in-gauge lines had a tendency to weave and wobble, due to their high centre of gravity, and the position of the train travelling above the lines. Brunel's proposal was to build a wider, 7ft-gauge line, where the engine and carriages did not so much travel above the rails as between them, with a lower centre of gravity, creating a more stable train, capable of faster speeds.

The planned line from Bristol to London was an extremely ambitious project, with multiple challenges ahead. It would be the longest continuous railway at the time, being nearly 120 miles long, and included building two bridges over the Thames, and a viaduct over the River Brent. The work would also include the building of Box Tunnel, nearly two miles of passageway through Box Hill between Bath and Chippenham, the building of which would take two and half years to complete. It was dug by navvies who accessed the tunnel via shafts cut down through the rock, and who used explosives to carve out the structure of the tunnel. Around a tonne of candles were used every week in lighting the work, and it is thought that 100 men died during its construction.

Brunel designed the various structures to be beautiful additions to the countryside, rather than utilitarian eyesores. He wanted to make the whole journey a wonderful experience for the middle and upper classes, and he needed to do so in order to obtain agreement from the many landowners over whose property the line would run. Not everyone was happy about the prospect, however. The Provost of Eton College, for instance, went to the Court of Chancery seeking to prevent the company from stopping any trains within three miles of the college for fear that the boys would be continually hopping on the train to enjoy the distractions of London.

The London and Birmingham Railway used the standard-gauge track (4ft 8½in) and were unhappy about sharing a Euston terminus with the GWR, so in December 1835 the GWR decided to buy land in Paddington for their London station, and in 1838 a temporary station was opened at the brick viaduct known as the Bishops Road Bridge, where the plat-forms were covered by a basic wooden structure, and waiting rooms were built into the arches of the bridge.

In February 1836 work started on the impres-sive Wharncliffe viaduct in Hanwell, London, over the River Brent. This was named after Lord Wharncliffe in gratitude for his services in carrying their Act of Incorporation through the House of Lords. The viaduct was built in Brunel's favourite Nubian Egyptian style, with nine brick arches, with Lord Wharncliffe's armo-rial bearings centred over the middle column, carved in stone. The whole structure was truly a wonderful piece of architecture and a great tribute to both Wharncliffe and Brunel.

On 31 May 1837 the GWR ran its first train, pulled by the *North Star*, running from London to Maidenhead, carrying directors and guests, with Brunel on the footplate. It is said that such was the excitement generated by this milestone that on the return journey one of the directors, Thomas Guppy, ran along the tops of the carriages in sheer excitement, as the train reached speeds of up to 33mph.

GWR's passenger service started on 4 June 1838 with varied success, and on 7 January 1839 GWR shareholders voted to continue using broad gauge, amid speculation from investors that broad gauge was not working very well. In fact the gauge was not the problem. Brunel took it upon himself to design his own engines, which unfortunately were underpowered, so much so that they laboured terribly under the strain of pulling coaches.

He had also redesigned the track with longer gaps between the sleepers, and wooden supports under the rails. These were held down by deep piles holding the track to the ground. However, the resulting track proved to be far too rigid, giving a bumpy ride for passengers, and poor performance in terms of train speed. The track was eventually pulled up and relaid, allowing it to 'give', or yield slightly, under the strain of carrying the heavy locomotives. Brunel's young Loco-motive Superintendent, Daniel Gooch, strug-gled to get Brunel's engines to run well, and the service had to rely on two traditional engines – the *North Star* and the *Morning Star* – which Gooch had bought for the company, before the GWR finally gave in and bought a fleet of better designed engines built by Robert Stephenson & Company.

In 1839 the Chief Inspector of the Great Western Railway Police was having his own problems, after a letter had been published in *The Times* accusing him of 'locking up' a child of ten years old for picking flowers on the slopes at Paddington Station, more commonly known as 'The Lawn'. In his defence he wrote to the editor vindicating his conduct, stating that he was not so ignorant as to lock anyone up in something other than a Metropolitan Police Station House, and that the girl in question did not pick a single wallflower as reported, but a 'tolerable handful'. He added that, far from being locked up and much terrified, the girl was merely taken, with her friends, to the Female Housekeeper's Room where she was cautioned not to offend in like manner again, and released after three to five minutes, 'no harsh or intimidating language whatever having been made use of from first to last'. He added that the slopes were maintained at considerable expense by the company, and yet they found people constantly trampling them down and wantonly destroying the plants and flowers.

The GWR had run trains on sections of the line for four years, but it must have been a relief for Brunel when, on 30 June 1841, the first train made its way along the entire line, all the way from Paddington to Bristol.

Problems at Paddington Station

In common with stations the world over, lost property began to be an issue at Paddington Station. In August 1841 a handbill was distributed offering a reward of two sovereigns for property lost between Paddington and Tottenham Stations: a dressing case and a carpet bag. The handbill said that whoever returned the items would receive the reward from the Rev. W Gaussen, 3 King's Bench Walk, Temple [London]. The following month, however, Mr William Gaussen, who had worked with the GWR on legal issues previously, and who had finally seen one of the flyers, complained to the company, saying that he realized they had been asked to print these unreasonable bills, but it was not their role to do so, and no more should be printed. 'It is rather unfortunate that a "Reverend" is placed before my name, which might serve many persons to justify a sneer, but I notice the accident merely to show the inconvenience of persons undertaking to advertise for complete strangers.'

Life at the Bishops Road Bridge station was getting busier. It was here that Queen Victoria alighted after her first train journey on 13 June 1842, travelling from Slough after a trip to Windsor Castle. She was fascinated by the new machinery, and wanted to examine the train instead of resting in her waiting room. Prince Albert, however, had been rather startled by the speed of the train, which would have been an average of 43 miles per hour, and he asked the driver to take it somewhat more slowly next time. The GWR subsequently fitted a signal to the roof of the royal saloon so that the driver could be notified if the royal party felt that the train was travelling too fast.

The New Paddington Station

By 1850 it was becoming obvious that the terminus at Bishops Road Bridge, with its four platforms and wooden roof, was inadequate, and in December Brunel quickly drew up plans for the new Paddington Station. He knew that he wanted something grand and majestic, built to his own design and highly engineered with a soaring metal roof, but he needed input from someone experienced in the fine detail of ornamentation. So in January 1851 he wrote, in quite an earnest manner, to the Secretary of the Royal Commission for the Great Exhibition, architect Matthew Digby Wyatt, offering him the chance to work on the finer details of his new station at Paddington. Impressed by the Crystal Palace built in Hyde Park for the Great Exhibition of 1851, Brunel designed his station on similar lines, with an iron and glass roof, but leaving the finer decorative details to Digby Wyatt. Brunel wanted Paddington to be a statement, showcasing his railway, and to be more impressive than the Great Northern Railway's Euston Station.

The engineering company Fox, Henderson and Company, led by Charles Fox, already specialized in railway construction, but had also worked on the Crystal Palace, the huge plate glass and iron structure build in Hyde Park to house the Great Exhibition of 1851 – a world showcase of technology and invention. Brunel wanted his own version of this building, and he awarded the company the contract to make the wrought-iron sections for his new station, while the roof was to be made from Paxton glazing, designed by Joseph Paxton, and using the same system as in the Crystal Palace. The original Paxton glass roof panels were only replaced in the 1990s when the glass was replaced by polycarbonate panels.

Brunel designed the station roof to comprise three arches, with a combined width of 240 feet. The length of the roof had to be 700 feet, so as to cover the complete of length of the platforms and trains. The centre span was to be 102 feet 6 inches wide, and 54 feet in height. The outer spans were to be 69 feet 6 inches and 68 feet wide, with the whole station covering an area of eight acres. The roof was to include 189 wrought-iron arch ribs, with the centre half of each of the curved roofs being glazed, and the rest covered with corrugated galvanized iron. There were to be ten tracks in the station, five with platforms and five as shunting lines, all initially built as 7ft broad-gauge tracks, although a third rail was later installed, allowing for the use of both broad and standard gauges. It was not until 1892 that the last broad-gauge train left the station: the 'Cornishman' express train for Penzance, which pulled out of Paddington on 20 May 1892.

Alongside the platforms Brunel designed office buildings, with the traffic department using the lower floors and GWR management the upper floors. An additional suite of rooms was built for Queen Victoria to use on her anticipated trips to Windsor Castle. The overall cost of the station was £650,000, and on 16 January 1854 the first passenger train left the new Paddington Station – the station was finally open.

Horses were still used at this time for the routine shunting of waggons and the onward delivery of goods transported by rail, and not far from Paddington Station, located in Winsland Street, is the Mint Building. Originally owned by the GWR, this building was originally a stable housing up to 600 horses on three floors. Even today you can still see the steep ramps built on the outside, to enable horses to reach the upper floors. The building remained as stables until the 1950s, when it became a research laboratory; it is now part of St Mary's hospital, known as the Mint Wing.

The Great Western Royal Hotel

The Great Western Royal Hotel, located at the front of Paddington Station, was a separate concern designed by Philip Charles Hardwick on land previously used to shunt goods wagons. It was Brunel's idea to add the hotel, which was designed to resemble a French château. It was the first of the large impressive London railway hotels, with 103 bedrooms, a coffee room, a reading room, a billiard and smoking room, and apartments for families, and, like the GWR itself, its intended clientèle were to be of the highest order. GWR shareholders were approached in January 1853 with a view to forming an

Great Western Hotel. RAIL1014/37/8

The lounge of the Great Western Hotel from an undated photograph.   RAIL1014/37/8

association for the purpose of opening and running the hotel in an efficient manner. The directors aimed to raise the £15,000 needed by selling shares, and hoped to have the building completed in the summer of that year.

The hotel opened on 9 June 1854, and its frontage included a varied collection of classical sculptures by John Thomas located on the central pediment facing Praed Street. At each end of the hotel façade was an impressive square tower. Brunel's vision was that people would eventually be able to travel from London to New York on one ticket, staying at the hotel before travelling by train to Bristol, and then boarding his *Great Western* steamship to America.

Improvements and Developments in the Late 1800s

Paddington Station can also boast that it was the first Underground Railway terminus in the world. Technically this was at the Bishops Road end of the station, but nevertheless on 10 January 1863 the Metropolitan Railway opened its new line that ran from Paddington for 3.75 miles to Farringdon Street, a journey that took just eighteen minutes. Much of the line was actually underground, built using the cut-and-cover method of tunnel construction, and the track was laid with three rails, to allow the use of both the broad-gauge GWR rolling stock, and standard-gauge trains borrowed from the Great Northern Railway. A total of 38,000 passengers used the new service on its first day.

Among the strange things related to the station and still to be seen in Paddington today are two 'dummy houses' at 23 and 24 Leinster Gardens, Lancaster Gate. They were built by the Metropolitan Railway to cover up a gap between the houses created as a result of the track passing beneath this spot. The 'cut and cover' method of creating underground tunnels meant that

A Hospital for the Crimea

Never one to turn down an opportunity, Brunel accepted an invitation from Sir Benjamin Hawes, the Permanent Undersecretary at the War Office, in February 1855, to design a portable, prefabricated hospital for use in the Crimea. Britain had been involved in the Crimean War since 1854, and the barracks at Scutari, Turkey, had become the British Hospital out there. But poor conditions meant that diseases such as dysentery, cholera, typhoid and malaria were rife, and Florence Nightingale campaigned for the British Government to send aid to improve conditions. Hawes wanted Brunel to design a prefabricated hospital ward that could be built in Britain and then shipped out to Turkey. Brunel took up the challenge and worked extremely fast on the project. Within six days a prototype ward was ready, built, and put on display at Paddington Station. By May of 1856 the finished wards had arrived in Erenkoy, Turkey, where they were unpacked and put together, ready for the first 300 patients by July, with sixty of the wards forming the new Renkioi Hospital for British troops.

the original houses were destroyed, and a false façade was created to make it look as though the two houses were still there. Even today it is hard to tell that the houses are not real, although the windows are painted on, and there are no letterboxes in the doors.

Keeping the approach roads to the station clean and tidy was highly desirable to the Great Western Railway, and they were willing to pay contractors to clear away rubbish and horse manure from outside the premises. In 1867 a Mr John Peters signed an agreement with the GWR to wash down the roads outside the station three times a day (and once on Sundays), and to 'cart away all scrapings, dust, straw or other rubbish' for forty shillings per week. Not to miss out on profitable manure, his contract also stated that he must pay five shillings per week to the GWR for the dung and rubbish carted away. Presumably they expected him to be able to sell the manure on to third parties.

Electric lighting was introduced to Paddington Station in 1880, powered by its own generating plant. On the first day of operation one of the messenger boys was so excited about the new innovation that he switched on every light as he walked down the long corridor from the Board Room to the Superintendent's Office. As he reached the end of the corridor he turned round to see the full effect and realized that a man had been walking behind him switching the lights off again. Undaunted, the boy ran back and switched them all on again. Although he did not know it, the man behind him had been Sir Daniel Gooch, Chairman of the GWR, and although the Superintendent wanted the boy sacked, Gooch merely remarked, 'Well, well. Boys will be boys.'

Railway companies liked to cultivate a loyalty and unity amongst staff, encouraging the formation of clubs and societies, and newsletters were published that served to promote the feeling of a company family. In January 1889 a new staff magazine was printed for 'private circulation only'. Its title was *The Josser*, meaning a circus entertainer, a simpleton or fool. Priced at one penny, the headline in the first edition was 'A Miscellany of Rubbish'; it was edited by E. A. Searson. It was available to the staff of the Paddington Goods Station and they were encouraged to send in poems, jokes and articles to be published. Its tone was quite satirical and self deprecating, with articles on, for

example, the weight and drinking habits of the
various groups of Paddington staff, racing tips,
and news on up-coming concerts and dinners.
Its first edition celebrated its own birth with
a poem:

> There was joy and jubilation, when unto the
>   British nation,
> A whisper had been carried from afar,
> That a journal had been started, and some
>   learned men had parted,
> Their allegiance from the *Echo* and the *Star*;
> To help in circulating every scrap of news
>   worth stating,
> And retail it to *The Josser*, for a charge
> That very clearly hinted, that the whole
>   affair was printed
> For the good of the Community at large.
>
> Perhaps we'd better mention, it's the
>   Editor's intention
> To continue our appreciated Skits,

> It's a fact too most important, 'though we
>   says it p'raps as oughtn't,'
> It will knock all other papers into fits.
> Narratives not too exotic, Statesmen's
>   speeches patriotic
> We'll insert them without any extra charge,
> We'll give tips to lovers courting, and
>   advice on matters sporting,
> For the good of the community at large.
>
> So Democrats and Tories, if you're wanting
>   wholesome stories
> And information interspersed with fun,
> Pay up your contribution to this
>   journal Lilliputian,
> It's the best that you will find beneath the sun.
> No longer be delaying, for the price that
>   you are paying,
> Remember is the very smallest charge
> We're justified in making for this
>   glorious undertaking,
> For the good of the Community at large.

The last broad-gauge train to Cornwall, 1892. COPY1/409

Royal Funerals

Paddington Station has seen the final journeys of four monarchs over the years, as each funeral party has travelled from the station to Windsor. The usual pattern for a royal funeral is that the coffin is carried to Westminster Hall where it lays in state for a period of three days, draped with the Royal Standard. The coffin is then transferred by gun carriage, pulled by sailors of the Royal Navy, as part of a long

Arrival of churns of Milk, Paddington Station

The 'milk train' to Paddington.
RAIL253/76

'Platform 7'.
RAIL253/80

Holiday crowds at Paddington Station.
August 1929.

Holiday crowds at Paddington. RAIL253/76

procession including state officials and foreign dignitaries, to Paddington Station, from which it is taken by train to Windsor. The final burial takes place in St George's Chapel, at Windsor Castle.

Queen Victoria's funeral cortège left Paddington on 2 February 1901, her coffin having arrived at Waterloo following the journey up from the Isle of Wight, where she passed away. She asked that there should be no lying in state, and that it should be a military-style funeral, which has set the standard for subsequent royal funerals ever since. The funeral train of King Edward VII left on 20 May 1910, his coffin having been followed in the procession by his faithful fox-terrier named Caeser.

The body of King George V was also taken by train to Windsor on 28 January 1936, after a period of lying state, with his four sons standing guard next to the coffin: the 'Vigil

Queen Victoria's
funeral procession.
RAIL253/31

Two diesel express
trains entering
Paddington in
1960. MT124/50

Paddington 'events board'. RAIL253/76

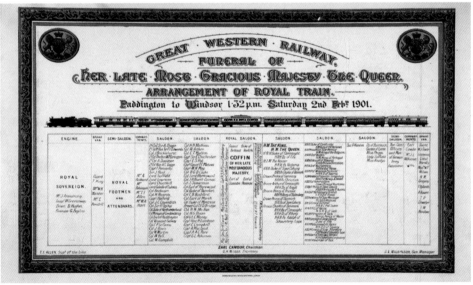

The Royal Train for Queen Victoria's funeral. RAIL253/31

of the Four Princes'. The fourth monarch was King George VI, whose train left Paddington for Windsor on 15 February 1952. In 2002 the remains of his widow, Queen Elizabeth the Queen Mother, and the ashes of his daughter Princess Margaret, were also interred alongside his body in St George's Chapel.

Improvements and Events in the 1900s

The structure and layout of a main line railway station can never be said to be finished, and there will always be continual repairs, re-structuring and improvements being made. Between 1906 and 1915 the station was enlarged with the addition of three more platforms covered by a new fourth span, built in a similar style to the original three, but lacking some of the more intricate decoration. At the same time Brunel's original iron columns were gradually replaced by steel ones, which took until 1924 to complete.

On platform 1, about halfway down, stands the Great Western Railway war memorial, which takes the form of a bronze statue of a soldier reading a letter from home. The figure was created by Charles Sargeant Jagger, the accomplished sculptor who also created the Royal Artillery memorial in Hyde Park. The Paddington memorial was unveiled on 11 November 1922 at a ceremony attended by Viscount Churchill, Chairman of the GWR. The memorial bears the following inscription: 'In Honour of those who served in the Great War 1914 + 1918'. It continues: '25,479 men of the Great Western Railway joined his Majesty's forces – 2,524 gave their lives'. A roll of the names of those who died was deposited in a casket beneath the bronze figure.

Further large-scale improvements to Paddington Station were implemented in 1933 when the number of platforms was increased to sixteen, and the area behind the hotel known as 'The Lawn', on which flowers and rhubarb were originally grown, was roofed over and became a passenger concourse.

During World War II, part of the Departure Side buildings was demolished by enemy action in 1941. On 21 March 1944 a large German bomb crashed through the roof over platforms 6 and 7, causing a fifty-foot crater. Platforms 3 to 8 were temporarily closed, and the station master was forced to take over the Queen's waiting rooms to use as his office.

Paddington Station was the scene for a heroic act of bravery on 9 March 1949. At 7am police

Return of the City of London Imperial Volunteers (CIV), Paddington 1900. RAIL253/31

constable Thomas Godwin was on duty in Praed Street when he saw two heavy draught horses pulling a railway van galloping from the exit road at the station into Praed Street. Noticing that there was no driver, forty-five-year-old Godwin ran into the roadway alongside the horses and managed to grab hold of the reins with his left hand, and the draughts chain with his right hand. Lifted from his feet at times he kept tugging at the reins, trying to stop the 15cwt horses, and after struggling with the horses for about fifty yards he was able to bring them to a standstill. Godwin strained the muscles of his left shoulder and was unable to return to work for twenty-seven days, but was awarded a commendation and a payment of £15 from the Bow Street Metropolitan Magistrates Court Reward Fund for his action in averting a serious accident.

Today a plaque can be seen on the wall near platform 1, installed in 1954 to mark the centenary of the station opening, and Brunel's balcony can be seen halfway up the wall next to the same platform. This wrought-iron structure shows the site of his office, and is not far from the life-size bronze statue of Brunel, shown sitting holding his trademark top hat, created by John Doubleday in 1982.

Paddington Station Today

Much of the traffic through Paddington Station is now commuter based, although the sunny holiday destinations of Devon and Cornwall can still be reached by train from here too. According to the Office of Rail and Road, Paddington is the UK's seventh busiest station, with 35,724,684 passengers coming and going every year. And the station is still evolving. Paddington Station will be part of the new Crossrail line running from Reading in Berkshire, and Heathrow Airport in the west of London, through to Shenfield in Essex in the east. The section between Paddington and Abbey Wood in the east will be joined by an underground line known as the Elizabeth line, due to open in December 2018. ✿

Chapter 7

VICTORIA, 1860

VICTORIA STATION AS WE SEE IT TODAY is actually the result of two separate railway stations that were built right next to each other. During the late 1850s several railway companies vied for access to the lucrative West End of London. They could see that creating access to the wealthy areas to the west of the city was likely to prove a profitable investment, and many began planning extensions to their lines, with termini in the most affluent parts of London. The railway companies serving the south and south-east coast all terminated south of the Thames, making it difficult for residents and businesses on the north side of the Thames to travel south. These companies therefore started to plan for termini north of the

A depiction of the façade of Victoria Station in 1904. RAIL414/554

The site of Victoria Station can be seen at the bottom of this map of the area in 1799, by R. Horwood. MR1/682

river, giving access to the affluent West End, the businesses in the City of London and the residential areas of north London.

The New Victoria Station

In 1857 the idea of an independent terminus to the north of the Thames for the use of multiple railway companies based in the south of England was discussed, and this was known as the 'Grosvenor Terminus'. On 23 July 1858 the new Victoria Station and Pimlico Railway Company (VS&PR) was formed, set up as a joint enterprise between four railway companies, mainly to oversee the development of an extension from the existing London, Brighton and South Coast Railway (LBSCR) terminus at Battersea,

across the Thames to a new terminus towards Pimlico. The four companies involved were the Great Western (GWR), the London and North Western (LNWR), the East Kent Railway (EKR, soon to become the London Chatham and Dover Railway – LCDR) and the LBSCR. German-born Leopold Schuster, Chairman of the LBSCR, and Thomas Wingate Henderson were appointed directors of the new VS&PR company.

Since the LBSCR had provided half of the capital for the project they were entitled to one side of the station, while the other half would be leased to the LCDR and the Great Western jointly. The site chosen was the old Grosvenor Canal Basin, which provided the cheapest location in the area, which was purchased from the Marquis of Westminster. The new station was to be called Victoria, after Victoria Street, which runs next to the site, and the engineer in charge was to be Sir John Fowler, who later went on to build London's first underground railway, the Metropolitan Railway, as well as the Forth Railway Bridge, near Edinburgh.

The LBSCR side of the station, known as the Brighton Side, opened on 1 October 1860, although there was quite a lot of opposition from local residents who feared that pollution from soot, dirt and noise would have a detrimental effect on their lives and properties (this was a wealthy area, after all). In order to get parliamentary permission to build the station an amendment was made to the plans to include the building of a large steel and glass roof enclosing the tracks north of the Thames and into the station. The additional expense of what to all intents and purposes would be a tunnel, meant that the usual impressive station frontage, which all London stations tended to have, had to be forfeited, and instead a simple wooden palisade was constructed, which actually lasted for forty years. It was another two years before the LCDR side of the station, known as the Chatham Side, opened, on 25 August 1862.

The new Victoria Station required the building of a bridge over the Thames – the Grosvenor Bridge, which was built between 1859 and 1860 and cost £84,000; Sir John Fowler was the engineer. Also known as Victoria Railway Bridge, this was London's first dedicated railway bridge, and it carried two lines into Victoria Station. The first stone of the new bridge was laid on 9 June 1859, and exactly a year later the first locomotive used the new bridge to cross from one side of the Thames to the other. Due to the immediate popularity of the station the bridge was widened between 1865 and 1866 to take an additional four lines, and a seventh line was built in 1907. This lasted until 1963, when the whole bridge was rebuilt with ten separate spans, each carrying its own railway track; by 1968 it was the busiest railway bridge in the world, carrying 1,000 trains each day.

The Grosvenor Hotel

In common with other London stations a large and luxurious hotel was built nearby. The Grosvenor Hotel was constructed along the western side of Victoria Station on the Buckingham Palace Road, built by Sir John Kelk, MP and public works contractor, and designed by the architect James Thomas Knowles, who specialized in designing large country houses for the gentry. It was a lavishly designed hotel for wealthy guests, built to impress with its French-style roof and Italianate façade. The hotel opened in 1862, and although it was accessible from the station, it was privately owned and had no formal connection to either the LCDR or the LBSCR. It was the first London hotel to feature a lift, which they called an 'ascending room'.

The two halves of the station had separate entrances, and each half had its own character. The Brighton side, run by the LBSCR, was regarded as superior to the Chatham side, the clientèle being the middle and upper classes travelling to the country or the south coast, for entertainment and high living. The Chatham side, run by LCDR, was much more working class, their trains taking dockworkers and merchant seamen to the east end of London and the Chatham docks.

In the year 1870 several alterations and improvements were made at Victoria, and in 1878 the subway down to the Metropolitan District underground station was constructed; but generally speaking the station remained substantially the same during the first forty years of its life. Both sides of the station provided for holiday trips, and the LCDR introduced the 'Family Saloon' in 1881, a special coach which could be hired for family events. It had both first and second class compartments, so that wealthy families could bring their servants with them on holiday. The carriage was fitted out with toilet facilities, and included a large saloon in the centre of the coach for parties or family gatherings.

A Powerful Explosion

On 26 February 1884 Victoria Station suffered a powerful explosion. Witnesses said that it sounded like a cannon being fired. A small fire broke out due to several broken gas pipes, although the night watchmen soon extinguished the flames. Luckily the station had been closed for the night and very few people were present. Only two people were injured by the explosion: a night porter named Kattan and a passing tinsmith named Fulford, who rushed into the station to see if he could help. They were both injured by falling debris.

The explosion occurred in the cloakroom of the LBSCR side of the station, and was so powerful that railings next to the steps to the subway were blown down, the walls between the cloakroom, the ticket office and the waiting room were blown to pieces, causing the roof to collapse, leaving a scene of complete destruction. The floor of the cloakroom was found to be littered with the charred wreckage of luggage bags, packages, pieces of wood and plaster. Several buildings outside the station were also damaged, including the Shakespeare and the Windsor Castle public houses.

Following an investigation by Her Majesty's Chief Inspector of Explosives, Colonel V. D. Majendie CB, a report was submitted to Parliament in which the cause of the explosion was put down to approximately 20lb of dynamite, which had been deliberately left at the station – a bomb. Investigations at other railway stations in London the following night led to the discovery of similar home-made bombs at Paddington, Charing Cross and Ludgate Hill stations, though thankfully none of these had actually exploded.

The devices were all made in the same way, and consisted of a large portmanteau travel bag packed with forty-five slabs of dynamite arranged around a metal tin containing an American 'Peep O'Day' alarm clock, made by the Ansonia Clock Company. On the back of the clock a small waistcoat or vest-pocket pistol had been wired, and arranged in such a way as to fire when the clock's winding handle moved round on the trigger. Opposite the barrel of the pistol were seven detonators, pushed into the dynamite. The clocks, the pistols, the cartridges and the dynamite all appeared to be American in origin.

Two of the bombs had failed to explode because the pistols had miss-fired. The third bomb, the one found at Paddington Station, had not exploded due to a small metal stud on the back of the clock preventing the winding handle from reaching the trigger. However, after the timing device had been removed from the explosive it was taken home by one of the investigating officers, and the jolting involved in transporting the clock freed up the winding handle and the pistol fired itself harmlessly during the night!

It was later established that the bombs were planted by supporters of the Irish Republican

Brotherhood, a Fenian organization that sought to bring about an Irish Republic, led by Jeremiah O'Donovan Rossa while he lived in exile in the USA. It was he who arranged a bombing campaign against British targets, mainly in London, from 1881 to 1885.

A Major Improvement Programme

Between 1902 and 1908 a major improvement programme was implemented at Victoria Station, at a cost of £2 million. It was becoming obvious that the station premises were struggling to cope with the rapidly expanding traffic of the railway, and powers had been obtained from Parliament in 1899 to enlarge the Brighton side of the station. Constricted by the Chatham side of the station on one side, and Buckingham Palace Road on the other, an innovative plan emerged to lengthen the platforms so that they could accommodate two trains at once, and yet leave each train free to leave the station. Each platform would now have a north and a south section, each half capable of accommodating a separate train, and thereby doubling the capacity of the station.

The reconstruction work involved the complete demolition of the property next to Buckingham Palace Road, totalling eight acres in area, to accommodate the expansion of the station and the hotel. The land was soft and damp, originally being part of the Grosvenor Basin and canal, itself carved from soft London clay, so major work was required to provide adequate foundations for the new buildings. A total of 1,200 wooden piles were driven into the ground, made from American pine, each fourteen inches square and between thirty-eight and forty-five feet in length, to provide support for the new hotel annexe.

The wooden palisade along the northern façade of the station was finally replaced by a baroque or renaissance-style frontage, with Portland stone dressings and an impressive clock in the centre. A glass awning was provided along the front of the station to provide protection from the elements for those entering or leaving their carriages, while twenty elevators were installed in the station and the Grosvenor Hotel by the Easton Lift Company, at a cost of £5,907 (and 13s).

A magnificent new train departure indicator board was also installed at this time. It allowed for the times, platform numbers and final destinations of up to eighteen trains to be displayed, each having its own clock showing the departure time, and up to twenty stopping stations per train. The names of the stations were printed on 360 octagonal rollers, worked by geared handles, and the whole board was said to be the largest in the world at that time.

The Funeral of King Edward VII

Victoria Station was the arrival point for European royalty when many foreign dignitaries arrived for the funeral of King Edward VII on 20 May 1910. This involved a vast procession from Buckingham Palace to Westminster Hall, where a brief ceremony took place, after which the funeral cortège continued on through London to Paddington Station, where the body of the King was taken by train to Windsor. This occasion saw the largest gathering of European royalty ever to occur, with seven kings, three queens, twenty-eight princes and ten princesses, almost all of them actually related to the late King.

A majestic stone archway was also built, spanning the entrance roadway from Buckingham Palace Road into the station. This was added with the royal family in mind, who could now enter the station conveniently under the arch and board their train at either platform 7 or 8, without having to use the public entrance.

The work had seen the station double in size to sixteen acres, all overseen by the Chief Engineer to the LBSCR, (Sir) Charles Langbridge Morgan, who later went on to serve in the Royal Engineers during World War I, and the Territorial Army Engineer and Railway Staff Corps. As if to celebrate the introduction of the new facilities at the station, when the work was completed a new first class, all Pullman coach train was introduced, travelling from Victoria to Brighton. It was called the 'Southern Belle', later known as the 'Brighton Belle', and comprised palatial rolling stock, specially constructed for this service; it took exactly an hour to reach Brighton, leaving Victoria at 11am and returning at 5.45pm.

Electrification was introduced in around 1910, initially by overhead cable, and in 1923 by a third rail; the VS&PR was eventually absorbed into the Southern Railway at the grouping. All this time the two halves of Victoria Station had operated independently, with an eighteen-inch-thick brick wall standing between them, and it was only in 1924 that the newly formed Southern Railway arranged for the dividing wall to be opened up to allow movement from one station to the other. The platforms were re-numbered, finally acknowledging that the station was one entity, although many facilities were still duplicated in each half of the building.

The staff store at Victoria Station, 1918. RAIL 414/554

Train Services Provided

Whilst depending on the ordinary working commuter class for the bulk of their income, the railway companies always tried to associate themselves with the upper classes, offering luxury travel, exotic destinations and special services for those who could afford them. One such service was introduced on 15 May 1929, when the *Golden Arrow* train commenced its role as the British version of the French *Flèche d'Or*. Luxury first class travel between Paris and Calais had been provided in France since 1926 by the *Flèche d'Or*, and the Southern Railway realized that a similar service from London's Victoria Station to Dover would complete a lucrative link between the two capital cities. The *Golden Arrow* train comprised ten first class Pullman coaches, hauled by a Lord Nelson class locomotive. The journey to Dover took just over an hour and a half, enabling a complete journey from London to Paris to take six hours and thirty-five minutes.

Except for the period of World War II, the service continued in various forms, with first and second class coaches running right up until September 1972; the French counterpart *Flèche d'Or* had not run since June 1969. On its final journey from Victoria Station George Longley, the *Golden Arrow*'s driver for the preceding six years, did not seem particularly sentimental over losing this iconic piece of railway history, saying: 'It doesn't mean a thing to me. One train is just like another as far as I'm concerned.'

From 1936 Victoria Station provided an additional international service, being the starting point for the Continental Night Ferry, also known as 'Compagnie Internationale des Wagons-Lits et des Grands Express Européens'. This service comprised six British coaches and six sleeping cars of the Wagon-Lits Company, followed by three French SNCF brake vans. The train would be pulled by two Pacific steam engines, later replaced by a single electric locomotive, to Dover, where the French coaches would be transferred on to the Dunkirk ferry for their onward journey to Paris or Brussels.

Air-Raid Shelters During World War II

During World War II, air-raid shelters were installed on the platforms at the station, for the protection of staff and passengers during the Blitz. However, since they were technically on private property, despite being for the use of the general public, there was some disagreement between the City of Westminster Council and the Southern Railway as to who should have responsibility for maintaining the shelters, for cleaning them, and who should undertake the necessary stewardship roles. In August 1940 the Southern Railway maintained that it was the local authority's responsibility to provide

Lt Commander Mitinori Yosii, a Japanese attaché working for German intelligence, was covertly photographed at Victoria Station in June 1941. KV2/61

The station was the scene of an embarrassing international incident in October 1954, following the state visit of the Emperor of Ethiopia, His Imperial Majesty, Haile Selassie. The Emperor arrived at Victoria Station at 8.45pm ready to board the 9pm train to Paris, and as he stepped from his car a man in fancy dress standing behind a barrier four or five yards from Selassie raised his hand and started to speak in a loud voice. As he did so, a woman, also wearing unusual clothing, came past the barrier and presented some sort of address to the Emperor, who had stopped to take in the performance.

The Under Secretary of State for Foreign Affairs, John Hope, said later that he thought at first it might be some moving piece of Ethiopian ceremonial, but then a large elderly lady dressed as Britannia appeared and joined in with the bizarre performance. It then became apparent that the lines they were speaking were from Shakespeare's *Romeo and Juliet*, and the whole thing was unofficial and unplanned as far as the Foreign Office was concerned. A rather surprised Selassie turned to the Secretary of the Government Hospitality Fund to ask, 'What is this?' The quick-thinking Secretary replied, 'A group of Shakespearean actors, Your Majesty.' The Emperor then walked over to the actors and shook their hands.

The Foreign Office later discovered that the Ethiopian Embassy had sanctioned the performance, but had not informed the British authorities, much to the annoyance of John Hope, who wrote in the file on the incident: 'If the lady in the above case had plunged a knife into the Emperor we would have got the blame from public opinion...the man concerned had on one occasion shouted in front of Buckingham Palace that he had a valentine for the Queen. So he does not seem to be a very reliable character.'

and run the shelters. However, the shelters were located on the platforms – that is, beyond the point where the general public could access them without having already bought a train ticket – and it was the city council's role to pay for the protection of all members of the public, not just SR passengers and staff.

The council was adamant that the maintenance of the shelters in the station was beyond their remit, and that the station staff must look after them, and must steward the crowds of people who used them. A compromise was reached when the council suggested that station staff merely direct passengers to the shelters when required, and that a station policeman or foreman might look into the shelters occasionally to see that all was well. SR agreed to this, although they stubbornly refused to take responsibility for the care or first-aid needs of those using the shelters.

An Air Terminal for British United Airlines

Victoria Station, with its fast line to Brighton via Gatwick Airport, was the obvious choice for an airline check-in desk, and in 1962 an air terminal for British United Airlines (BUA) was built over platforms 15 and 16, enhancing the station's reputation for international travel. This was arranged by Freddie Laker, BUA's Managing Director, and £100,000 was spent on the new

London traffic outside Victoria Station, 1962–1964. HLG131/100

check-in desk, which enabled travellers to drop off their airline luggage before boarding the train to Gatwick Airport.

From May 1963 a twice-daily service was set up, harking back to the old *Golden Arrow* train-and-boat combination from London to Paris. This time a *Silver Arrow* train took international travellers from Victoria Station to Gatwick Airport, where a BUA Viscount aeroplane would continue their journey to Le Touquet, France, and from there a French SNCF train would take passengers to the Gare du Nord station in Paris. Although reasonably successful, the service was withdrawn in the late 1970s.

The Gatwick Express Service

On 10 May 1984 the Gatwick Express service began: a non-stop, high-frequency service from Victoria Station to Gatwick Airport, with a thirty-minute journey time and trains departing at fifteen-minute intervals. A new airport lounge was also provided at Victoria, together with airline check-in facilities. The service was launched with as much publicity as possible, pushing the international angle, following an opening ceremony at which the Lambeth Community Steel Band played, and a bottle of champagne was broken over the 'bow' of the new locomotive.

Airline hostesses were lined up next to the new train bearing lettered cards spelling out the words 'Gatwick Express', and specially invited guests were transported first class from Victoria to Gatwick, where they were greeted by the Hardin Simmons University Band from Abilene, Texas, an American suza band in cowboy dress, flown in by American Airlines. The guests, who included the Mayor of Crawley, the Lord Mayor of Westminster and many representatives of railway bodies and airline companies, then left the train and ascended the escalators to the airport itself, where a lavish lunch was provided and speeches given. Much was made of the fact that Gatwick was the only airport in the UK where a railway station was an integral part of the airport complex, and that passengers beginning their journeys from Victoria could now reach 120 destinations around the world via Gatwick airport.

Victoria Station Today

Today Victoria Station is the second busiest London Station after Waterloo, processing eighty-one million passengers every year. The original division between the two sides of the station is still evident from the destinations served by the nineteen platforms. The first eight platforms on the eastern side (the Chatham side) receive trains from Kent, while the western platforms (the Brighton side), numbered 9 to 19, serve the Brighton main line and the branch lines from Surrey, Sussex, Gatwick Airport and Brighton.

Chapter 8

CHARING CROSS, 1864

CHARING CROSS IS TRADITIONALLY held to be the location from which distances are measured to and from 'London.' But the two words in the name 'Charing Cross' have very different origins. 'Charing' is thought to be an anglicized version of the Anglo-Saxon word *ċerring* meaning 'bend', since the location is to the north of a bend in the River Thames. The 'Cross' element comes from the fact that, between 1291 and 1294, King Edward I had twelve crosses built, collectively known as Eleanor Crosses, in memory of his wife Eleanor of Castile following her death in 1290. Each of the twelve crosses marked a place where her body lay overnight on its journey down from Lincoln to London.

She was buried in Westminster Abbey, but the penultimate stop of the funeral procession was at the little hamlet of Charing, just to the south of today's Trafalgar Square, and the cross that was erected here was the most expensive and elaborate of the twelve, costing £650 as compared to £95 for the cross in Waltham Cross. It was made from marble and was located in what was then the Royal Mews. The cross was destroyed during the English Civil War and replaced in 1675 by a statue of King Charles I after the restoration of the monarchy. Hence the name 'Charing Cross', from which the railway station derives its name.

A Central West End Terminus

The South Eastern Railway (SER) already had a London terminus in the form of London Bridge Station, but during the early 1840s it became obvious to the company directors that they needed to make the most of their two major markets. Firstly there were the incoming commuters and passengers heading either for the City, or for the delights of London's West End. These people would arrive at London Bridge Station but then have to make their way across town through congested traffic. The second group were the wealthy out-going passengers going in the other direction, boarding trains at London Bridge Station and travelling down to Folkestone or Dover in Kent, on their way to the continent – a route for which the SER were in stiff competition with their rivals, the London, Chatham and Dover Railway.

If the SER could build a new terminus, to the north of the Thames, closer to the bright lights and wealthy residents of the West End, then they would be able to capitalize on both markets, and so maximize their profits.

By 1858 they had identified four possible locations for the new station: Charing Cross, York Road, Battersea and Pimlico. In a booklet published in support of the proposed new station, issued to the directors of the SER, each location

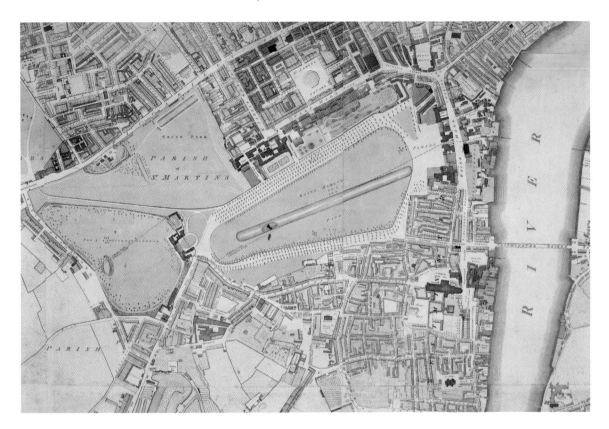

The site of Charing Cross Station in 1799 can be seen in the top left corner of this map by R. Horwood; Villiers Street survives to this day, but others have vanished under the modern station. MR1/682

was analysed, and it was clear that Charing Cross was the preferred option due to its location and a wide variety of other factors, but also because of the likely clientèle. The booklet explains that:

It is essential to remember that the population in the neighbourhood of Charing Cross is precisely of that character which will avail itself daily of railway communication with the suburbs of the metropolis, whilst the population in the York Road district is almost entirely composed of the poorest classes; and that the vicinity of Pimlico is inhabited chiefly by the more aristocratic classes, who, as is well known, travel by railway at certain stated times

of the year only… a central West End Terminus would be of much convenience to the highest classes of society – the nobility, gentry, members of Parliament, and their families, who principally reside at the West End of London – by enabling them to arrive in town during the season, and to leave it when it is over for their residences, or for sea-bathing quarters, or for the Continent, without passing through the crowded thoroughfares of the East End – and is, therefore, a most desirable accommodation.

The middle classes were also a target audience. The booklet outlines the imagined, and perhaps far-fetched, case of a father who has given his wife and family the benefit of country air for a month by placing them down in Reigate, Dorking or Tunbridge Wells, and contemplates visiting them two or three times a week from his residence in Regent Circus or Oxford Street. He knows he will be able to make the journey from London Bridge in only half an hour, but getting to London Bridge in the first place, across busy London, is the problem. Even if he puts himself to the 'objectionable expense of a cab', or takes an omnibus, he is likely to be held up in traffic, and so poor old 'Paterfamilias', being uncertain of his journey, abandons the whole idea, and the family stop at home, or they are sent elsewhere. How different it would be, dreams the narrator, if he could take his carpet bag and walk from his place of business to the station, able to depend on catching the train 'to a minute'.

The directors were convinced that Charing Cross was the correct location, and the SER set up a new subsidiary company, the Charing Cross Railway Company, which presented a bill to Parliament. Permission was granted on 8 August 1859 to build a new line from London Bridge Station towards Trafalgar Square, running 1½ miles through Southwark and Lambeth before heading north and crossing the River Thames. At the same time a new line would run from London Bridge to Cannon Street serving the City, and a third line linking Cannon Street with the new Charing Cross Station would be built, thus forming a triangle of tracks known as the Cannon Street Triangle.

The SER chose a site for the new station at the end of the Strand, not far from Trafalgar Square, occupied since 1682 by the Hungerford Market,

Charing Cross Station in 1891 showing the old station roof. COPY1/404

named after the aristocratic Hungerford family of Somerset who had owned the land since the 1400s. The market had never been a great success and was losing business to its strong competitors Billingsgate Market and Covent Garden, so in 1862 the SER bought the land and demolished the market buildings in order to build their new station. St Thomas's Hospital also required relocation, as did a number of graves from the burial ground of St Mary, Lambeth. Although it may have been an obvious choice to call it London's Hungerford Station, there was already a Great Western Railway Station by that name in the town of Hungerford, Berkshire, and so the SER chose to call it the Charing Cross Station.

The new station building was designed by Sir John Hawkshaw, engineer to the SER. He chose a simple design in the form of a large single span, trussed arched roof, covering the train shed, which included six platforms. Since the land sloped down from the Strand to the River Thames, the station needed to be built on a brick arched viaduct, which reached thirty feet in height at the southern end, although the entrance to the station was at ground level on the Strand. The roof above was 164 feet wide and 510 feet long, standing 102 feet at its highest point. The area underneath the viaduct was used for storing goods, including wine.

Hungerford Bridge

Rail access to the station was via a new bridge, also designed by Sir John Hawkshaw, called Hungerford Bridge. This replaced Isambard Kingdom Brunel's 1845 footbridge, a suspension bridge that included two impressive square Italianate towers, from which the road of the bridge was suspended by chains. This bridge had taken people from the South Bank over the river directly into Hungerford Market, although it is said that few people actually used it in summer due to the stench of the river at that time. Brunel's towers were demolished when the new bridge was built, although his two large buttress piers in the bed of the river were incorporated into the new design, and the chains were later used in the Clifton Suspension Bridge in Bristol.

Hawkshaw's new bridge was much criticized at the time for its lack of ornamentation, being a simple wrought-iron structure comprising nine spans across the Thames, carrying four railway tracks and a footpath on each side, twelve feet wide, secured in perpetuity for the free use of the public by the Metropolitan Board of Works. Hawkshaw's design was what is known in the engineering world as a 'pony truss' bridge, where the traffic moves through the supporting structure of the bridge; it is a design known for its strength. It was utilitarian, but some said it was ugly, especially in comparison with Brunel's suspension bridge, which by design appeared graceful and pleasing to the eye. However, the original bridge would never have taken the weight of four fully loaded trains passing at the same time.

The look of the bridge has improved recently due to two new footbridges being added, one to each side of the railway bridge, suspended from steel pylons and cables, a millennium project opened in 2003, which was also the Queen's Golden Jubilee year.

Charing Cross Hotel

The obligatory railway hotel was built at the front of the station facing the Strand. Designed by Edward Middleton Barry, son of Charles

The Charing Cross Hotel, 1898. The building originally had an elaborate mansard roof, which can be seen in the photo. COPY1/437

Another view of the façade of the Charing Cross Hotel, 1899. COPY1/440

Barry, the architect who designed the House of Commons, it was opened in 1865 and comprised seven storeys, with 250 bedrooms. The hotel was large and impressive, and gave the station a French Renaissance frontage. It proved immediately popular and profitable, so much so that an additional ninety rooms were built in 1878 on the other side of Villiers Street, linked to the main hotel by a bridge over the street.

The hotel was, and still is, opulent, luxurious and substantial. The overall design was much more restrained than that of the St Pancras hotel, still grand and impressive but with less ornamentation, creating a feeling of serious dependability, class and timeless style. Originally it had a grey, French-style 'mansard' roof, that is, formed with two sets of rafters, the upper set inclining more than the lower set, and very common in Paris; however, this was replaced in 1951 by a new top storey, the walls of which were built from plain white brick.

Barry also designed a version of the Eleanor Cross, which stands in the hotel forecourt, re-imagined from the original that was destroyed by the Puritans in 1647. The monument is said to have inspired Queen Victoria to arrange for the erection of the Albert Memorial, to the memory of her consort. Barry based his design for the new monument on the only three drawings of the original cross that still survive, held in the British Museum, the Bodleian Library and the Society of Antiquaries.

Built from Portland stone, with the upper panels carved from red Mansfield, it stands seventy feet high and is more elaborate that the original cross. There are eight crowned statues, four of which show Eleanor as Queen, while the other four show her exercising charity, distributing bread and money, and founding churches. In the lower section are three shields, the designs for which are copied from the surviving crosses at Nottingham and Waltham. The location of the monument also serves to conceal the fact that the hotel was not built precisely parallel to the Strand, a deviation said to be most pleasing when viewing the building from Duncannon Street.

A Proposed New Road Bridge

In 1904 the London County Council considered buying the station from the South Eastern and Chatham Railway, and demolishing it in order to make way for a new road bridge linking the northern and southern tramway systems. A new station would have been built for the company on the south side of the Thames at the end of Hungerford Bridge – but the expense of such a large scheme prevented it from going ahead. Interestingly, this idea has been resurrected by Network Rail more recently, and included in their plans for railway lines between Kent and London issued in 2017, mainly due to the fact that the platforms at Charing Cross Station cannot accommodate twelve-car trains. The plans under discussion include a possible Blackfriars-style bridge station, extending over the Thames and down to Waterloo. Whether this comes to pass we shall have to wait and see.

The Roof Collapses in 1905

One defining moment in the life of the station occurred on 5 December 1905. Work was being carried out on the roof of the station, and around thirty men were involved. Gradually, one by one, the men began to realize that the enormous roof was changing shape and beginning to sag in the middle. Luckily there was enough time to clear the station platforms of staff and passengers, before the whole roof finally collapsed, with a tremendous boom. It seems that one of the important wrought-iron tie-rods had snapped, and a large section of Hawkshaw's roof was no more.

Reports state that the disaster took the lives of three station workmen, and the falling girders caused a wall to collapse destroying the nearby Royal Avenue Theatre, killing another three people. The Theatre was subsequently rebuilt and opened as the Playhouse Theatre in 1907, its first performance being a sketch especially written by George Bernard Shaw for the opening night entitled 'The Interlude at the Playhouse'. The resulting enquiry into the disaster raised questions about the integrity of the original station roof, which was one large arched structure with no central support. A moving timber gantry was built in order to safely remove the remains of the roof, and the new roof, which was built the following year, was designed as a simple, utilitarian, flat ridge-and-furrow roof, held up by posts and girders.

Charing Cross Underground Station

Ironically, the roof collapsing at this time came at an opportune moment for the construction of the new Charing Cross, Euston & Hampstead Railway, an underground railway commonly known as the Hampstead Tube. The line had been completed as far as Trafalgar Square, and the company now wanted to build its terminus underneath the forecourt of the Charing Cross Hotel. Obviously, the hotel required the forecourt to remain intact to enable guests and tradesmen, cabs and delivery vans to access the

Charing Cross Underground Station, May 1949. WORK25/219

hotel, and up until this point the South Eastern and Chatham Railway (SECR, formed when the SER merged with the London, Chatham and Dover Railway in 1899) had refused permission for the forecourt to be dug up, although they were happy for the Hampstead Tube to build their terminus entirely from below ground.

This was going to be a difficult task, but plans were completed for the necessary tube station shafts to be driven upwards from the tunnels below, and the booking hall to be excavated beneath the forecourt surface. However, when the Charing Cross Station roof collapsed, the forecourt to the hotel was closed to the public, and excavation work from above was allowed to go ahead.

For three months the hotel forecourt was out of action, and during this time the Hampstead Tube Company was permitted to open up the forecourt, sink their shaft and build their Underground terminus from the surface. They were only allowed six weeks in which to do this, but they managed to sink the main shaft to a depth of seventy-three feet, a lift shaft built with its winding gear at the bottom rather than the top, due to lack of space. A steel girder roof was formed over the tube station, and the forecourt surface was re-laid on top of that in time for the re-opening of Charing Cross Station on 19 March 1906.

The remainder of the excavation work was completed after the roof was on, materials and equipment having been dropped down the shaft and carried away through tube tunnels. In 1937 the Hampstead Tube was renamed the Northern Line, and the terminus underneath the hotel forecourt is now called Charing Cross Station, no longer a terminus but one of fifty stations on the Northern Line.

Charing Cross Station a Century Ago

It is perhaps difficult for us to imagine what visiting a station would have been like a hundred years ago. How would it have been different, and what were the day-to-day issues dealt with by the railway companies at that time? One file held at the National Archives helps to illustrate some of these points. MEPO 2/1340 is a Metropolitan Police file concerning the use of cabs at Charing Cross Station. The SECR started to allow motor cabs into the station, via a side entrance, through an archway and up a ramp to the platforms, in order to collect passengers. This was to be particularly useful to those who had used their ships to cross the English Channel, and may therefore have significant luggage. Most cabs in 1910 were still horse-drawn, and the hotel forecourt at the front was used for the collection and dropping off of passengers.

To us this may sound like a reasonable development, but at that time there was no electric lighting in the station. The Metropolitan Police became concerned about the dangers of allowing motor vehicles into this confined space, and a report was drawn up following an inspection of the building:

Inside the dark arch where cabs enter from the street are two naked gas jets, always burning, while further along are incandescent gas lamps. At the bend from the arch is the lamp store where the lighted oil lamps are taken on trolleys to be put in the trains. Naked lamps are constantly used in the lamp rooms.

The report continues that the stairs are gas lit, and that employees are freely permitted to smoke cigarettes or pipes. The roadway under the arch was at a considerable gradient, with cabs having to park at an angle, with their wheels against the kerb to prevent them running backwards. Only the first or last cab in the queue could easily leave the roadway. Cab engines were switched off to reduce pollution, otherwise the air would have been intolerable, but in starting their engines the drivers would usually flood their carburettors, the surplus spirit spilling on to the road and pooling while it evaporated.

The police argued that in an area with restricted access and the potential for hundreds of people passing through, inflammable gases and naked flames in a confined space could lead to an explosion. The police therefore objected to the scheme, but the file shows that the SECR were reluctant to be told what to do on what was their private property. After much discussion they came to a compromise whereby motor cabs were called forward, as required, by means of a bell, having waited in ranks outside the station, thus reducing the possibility of explosions.

Charing Cross Station had become the main terminus for the SER, rather than London Bridge Station, and was the main departure point for boat train services to continental Europe. The travel firm Thomas Cook even set up an office on the corner of the hotel forecourt. Prior to World War I it was possible to travel from London to Paris in six and a half hours. It was also the main departure point for troops during the Great War, travelling to the Western Front, while wounded soldiers were brought back to Charing Cross before being relocated to hospitals around the country.

On 26 December 1918, following the end of the war, the United States President, Woodrow Wilson, met King George V at Charing Cross Station, before travelling by horse and carriage past various London landmarks to Buckingham Palace in a colourful victory parade. Charing Cross was decorated for the occasion, and the streets were lined by 20,000 soldiers, while church bells rang, cannons were fired and the general public cheered and celebrated the end of the war.

Fire Damage during World War II

During World War II both the railway station and the hotel were badly damaged more than once by enemy bombing. One particularly bad night was that of the 16/17 April 1941, when a shower of incendiary bombs caused numerous fires in the Strand and the surrounding area. At about 4.15am the London Fire Brigade were notified of a fire in the Charing Cross Hotel, and numerous small fires on Hungerford Bridge. The brigade was already stretched with most of their appliances tackling other fires, but a small team of temporary and auxiliary firemen arrived and began to confront the blazes.

At first they were armed only with one trailer pump – and shortly after they started work they were informed by an air-raid warden that a land mine was present on the bridge, lying across the railway lines on the downstream side of the bridge. In one spot the fire was within ten feet of the mine. Fire Station Officer George Watling positioned two manned hoses, one within fifteen yards of the mine, and the other back on the station platform, while he and auxiliary fireman Alfred Blanchard walked along the bridge dealing with the numerous smaller fires caused by the incendiary bombs. Watling later said, 'The fires were burning fiercely on the

Throughout the summer months of 1927 Charing Cross station was constantly in the newspapers, as a grizzly mystery caught the attention of the public. On Friday 6 May 1927 a man deposited a very heavy, large black trunk at the left-luggage office at Charing Cross Station. He was issued with a ticket receipt, but this was later found screwed up on the floor, and he left the station in the same cab in which he had arrived. The trunk remained there until the following Monday, when staff noticed a strange and nasty smell coming from it. Chief cloakroom clerk, Mr Glass, decided to force the trunk open, and found that it contained the dismembered body of a woman; her arms and legs had been severed, wrapped in brown paper and tied up with string.

The police were called and a murder investigation was launched. There were several other items in the trunk, including a duster with a tag marked 'Greyhound'. This was traced to the Greyhound Hotel, Hammersmith, where a Mrs Robinson was employed. Her husband happened to work as an estate agent in rooms close to where the taxi driver had picked up the mystery man with the trunk, and after further investigations, a man named John Robinson was traced and interviewed by the police.

Without much resistance he confessed to causing the death of Mrs Minnie Alice Bonati, and cutting up her body, claiming that she had followed him to his office and demanded money from him. When he refused to pay her, there was a scuffle and she fell into the fireplace banging her head and knocking herself unconscious. Robinson's defence lawyers maintained that she died from suffocation, her nose being blocked by the carpet or her clothing, but the jury preferred to believe that Robinson had held a cushion to her face until she was dead.

What may have swayed the jury was his admittance that he had gone to the trouble of purchasing brown paper, a large butcher's knife and a trunk in order to dispose of the body, instead of simply reporting the death as an accident. Sentenced to death for his crimes, Robinson was executed at Pentonville Prison on Friday 12 August 1927.

---

bridge and approaching the land mine. I, with the Branch, gave the mine an occasional drink to keep it cool.'

At about 5.00am Station Officer Arthur French arrived with an escape van (designed to rescue people from buildings using a long ladder) and a scratch crew of firemen, and they started to attack the fires from the other side of the bridge. French could see that three railway coaches, a signal box and the railway track were all well alight, and at one point while investigating he found himself on top of the land mine. Despite the danger all members of the crew worked fearlessly for more than four hours to prevent the fire from reaching the mine, which, had it exploded, would have destroyed the railway bridge, the pedestrian bridges and parts of the station and hotel.

Meanwhile in the hotel, Station Officer John Adlam and his crew were fighting the fire that had taken hold on the roof and the top two floors of the building. His men were aware of the mine being only 250 yards away, and had it gone off, in all likelihood they would have been killed – yet they worked unceasingly and managed to prevent the fire spreading further. In the early morning when the mine disposal officer arrived to defuse the bomb, the fire was still not completely extinguished, and it was only with considerable difficulty that Adlam was persuaded to leave the fire while the bomb was defused. In a statement after the event, the bomb disposal officer Lieut E O Gidden, RNVR, said:

> When I arrived at Hungerford Bridge I found about half a dozen firemen working within fifteen feet of the unexploded mine. This had already lost its filling plate, exposing the explosive to the naked fire, should it have reached it. I warned the men of their imminent peril but they seemed not to care a jot, and I had to order them away. They left with great reluctance. Even the vibration of the firemen's footfalls around this mine could have set it off, as we have already learnt to our bitter experience.

George Watling and Arthur French received the George Medal for their bold and fearless leadership that night, with four other crew members receiving the British Empire Medal; the remaining eight firemen were given Commendations by the Interdepartmental Committee on Civil Defence Gallantry Awards.

An Air-Space Development Project

Very little development was undertaken with regard to the station during the 1950s to 1970s. However, in the late 1980s and early 1990s the

The Playhouse Theatre and Charing Cross railway bridge, 13 May 1949. WORK25/218

station was transformed by an air-space development project above the station, known as Embankment Place. In this development the 1906 roof above the platforms was replaced by a floating concrete pad upon which nine floors of office space were built, with ground floor offices being built below the station itself.

Away from the platforms the station concourse keeps a glass roof, and some Victorian features have been retained, including a two-faced clock, while the Strand façade remains unchanged, being the hotel frontage. But from the river, or looking up from the South Bank, Charing Cross station appears as a modern office block, with only two clues as to its past structure: the two curved roofing structures, which hark back to Hawkshaw's original arched roof design, and the Hungerford Bridge, which continues to feed rumbling trains into the mouth of the station, as it has done since 1864. ✿

Chapter 9

CANNON STREET, 1866

ANNON STREET STATION IS EASILY recognized today from the south bank of the Thames by its two domed towers that stand proudly against the skyline on the north side of the river. Built by the South Eastern Railway (SER) as one of their London termini, construction of the station started in 1863. The SER had intended to open the station in July 1866, but the Board of Trade's Railway Department Inspecting Officer, Colonel Yolland, found that the signals on the River Bridge just outside the station were not in working order, and a mistake had been made in the system adopted at the signal box. Together with rubbish and scaffolding poles cluttering up the station entrance, this meant that opening was delayed by a couple of months until 1 September 1866.

Cannon Street itself is a road that runs parallel to the Thames right in the centre of London, from the monument to St Paul's Churchyard. It follows the route of an ancient riverside track, first recorded in 1183 as Candelewrithstret, or the street of Candle-Wrights, the whole area being known for the production of candles. The name evolved into Candlewick Street, spelled in various ways over time, until the London accent of the locals gradually shortened it to Cannon Street. Even today one of the City wards is known as Candlewick, its name taken from the same derivation.

The London Stone

An ancient landmark known as the London Stone once stood in the ground now fronting Cannon Street Station, and various legends and attributes have been associated with it, including that it was the point from which all distances in Roman Britain were measured. It has also been said that Druids used it in sacrificial offerings, and that the Anglo-Saxons used it in their ceremonies, such as the Modraniht or 'Mother Night', which was the celebration of the winter solstice centred around a boar's head, or perhaps Blod-Monath, or 'Blood Month', held in November, when animals were sacrificed to the gods, thereby providing meat for the winter months. Made from limestone, the surviving relic is thought to be merely a small section of the original monument, which was a tall pillar, rooted several feet into the ground. The stone is now housed in the Museum of London awaiting the completion of building work which will result in its return to 111 Cannon Street where it traditionally sat, opposite the station.

Station Construction and Design

Cannon Street Station was built on the site of a medieval 'Steelyard', also known as a 'Stilliarde' or 'Stalhof'. This was a self-governing enclave and home to some 400 German and Flemish

merchants, who lived here from *c.*1250 until 1598, until their expulsion from England by Queen Elizabeth. They were part of the Hanseatic League, which traded across northern Europe, and it is thought that the name 'steelyard' is derived from the steelyard weighing balance that was built to weigh imported goods as they were hoisted ashore from the river boats.

The station's matching twin towers, and the side walls that once held the roof, are all that remain of the original building, which was designed by Sir John Hawkshaw, who later designed the Severn Tunnel, a railway tunnel linking England and Wales running under the estuary of the River Severn, and J. W. Barry, who went on to design London's iconic Tower Bridge. The station towers are Grade II listed and built from yellow brick, with a plain channelled lower section and a more decorative upper section with a cornice and parapet, topped off with a square domed roof, a squat lantern and a spire.

Between and behind the towers was a 700 foot-long train shed, covered by a glass and iron roof, built as an impressive semi-circular arch. The station consisted of nine tracks and five spacious platforms. Besides being decorative, large water tanks were discovered inside the towers, and it is thought that these were used for replenishing the steam engines, or for powering the station's hydraulic systems.

The tracks emerge from the station between the towers, and are carried over the sloping ground towards the Thames by a huge viaduct comprising twenty-seven million bricks, and then on to the Cannon Street railway bridge across the river towards London Bridge Station to the east, and Charing Cross Station to the west. The bridge was built with public walkways on either side at the insistence of the local authorities, but these were never used, except by the railway for storage purposes. To the south of the Thames the tracks formed what was known as the Cannon Street Triangle, a complicated arrangement where three lines headed in a westerly direction towards Charing Cross Station, and four lines went east to London Bridge

Station, with a couple more lines to and from both of those stations, making the third side of the 'triangle'.

The signalling and points for these lines was necessarily complicated and completely inter-locked. One train entering or leaving Cannon Street would block seven or eight other lines, and it was impossible to signal a train forwards until every point was duly set, and every conflicting signal locked at 'danger'. An engine turntable was also provided at the engine depot adjoining the south side of Cannon Street Bridge.

An Italian-Style Hotel

At the Cannon Street end of the station an Italian-style hotel was built, which opened in May 1867; it was designed by E. M. Barry, who had already received acclaim for his design of the Royal Opera House in Covent Garden, or the 'Royal Italian Opera' as it was known at the time. The hotel formed the front of the station, its ground floor accommodating all the usual station functions, such as the ticket office and waiting rooms. The French-style roof of the hotel included a turret at each end, mirroring the towers facing the bridge across the river, and rows of chimneys, giving the overall impression of a French château.

Railway companies almost always built hotels as part of, or near to, their London railway stations, and the five-storey hotel at Cannon Street was the smallest of the London railway hotels. It was originally known as the City Terminus Hotel, but changed its name to the Cannon Street Hotel in 1879; it finally closed to paying customers in 1931. The building was then converted into offices and became known as 'Southern House'.

Enviable Public Lavatories

The public lavatories of the newly built Cannon Street station were looked upon with envy by the General Manager of rival station King's Cross in 1872. Mr Oakley wrote to the directors of the Great Northern Railway (GNR) extolling the virtues of offering lavatories and private closets for the use of the travelling public, charging a penny a time for the accommodation, and suggesting that this was a business opportunity worth exploring on the GNR. He explained that the lavatories at Cannon Street were super-vised by paid attendants, and that the company received the money paid by the customers. In July 1872 alone 14,062 customers had used the facilities at Cannon Street, resulting in £58.11.10 profit to the company.

To avoid the lavatory attendants pilfering the pennies an ingenious lock was used on the lavatory doors, designed and supplied by Joseph Bailey, patentee of his 'Registering Lock'. It worked by the attendant in charge having a key which opened the lavatory door, and in doing so a dial inside the lock caused an indicator to move halfway between two figures. When the door was opened again, from inside by the customer, the indicator completed the cycle and stopped at the next figure. At the end of the day the inspector would then check the figures on the locks, and the attendant would have to hand over the appropriate sum of money.

A Fatal Accident in 1878

Cannon Street station was the scene of a fatal accident on 4 July 1878, when the 8.05 train from Erith to Cannon Street arrived at platform No. 1. As the train was coasting at walking pace the door of the centre compartment of a third-class carriage opened, and a lady began to step out. This went against the usual procedures at the time, which were that railway staff would open the doors once the train had stopped moving. William Gallen, Platform Inspector, saw her and called out for her to wait until the train had stopped. Nevertheless, Mrs Weaver placed her right foot on to the continuous footboard, and then turned her body against the direction of the train to place her left foot on to the platform.

She immediately fell backwards on to the platform, and Gallen ran forward to assist. As she rolled towards the edge of the platform he managed to grab hold of her right arm, but her left arm was struck by the iron steps of the next carriage. Gallen was then knocked over by other passengers rushing over to see what was happening, and the lady fell into the gap between two carriages and down on to the rails.

The platform was less than three feet above the level of the rails, and the Board of Trade Railway Department Inspecting Officer, Colonel W. Yolland, in writing his report on the accident, stated that longer footboards along the sides of carriages, running to the buffer stocks, would have prevented the death occurring, since the gap between the carriages would have been too narrow to allow a body to fall through. He added that about fifty people died each year in a similar fashion. Tragically, Gallen's rescue attempt was to no avail, and Mrs Weaver died as the second carriage wheels ran over her head and neck.

Season Tickets for Routine Passengers

Regular travellers were the company's bread and butter, and a whole raft of season tickets was available to purchase covering travel between all, or certain stations, for periods ranging from one week to twelve months in duration. In this way the company promoted the routine use of the railway in the daily commute into London for

Paddle steamers on the Thames by Cannon Street Bridge, 1911. COPY1/555

thousands of passengers. In 1912 the cost of a first class annual season ticket for all stations to and from Cannon Street station was £75, and £60 for second class. However, the holder of such a ticket (assuming you were male) would be entitled to another 'lady's ticket' at half rate for 'the wife'.

A deposit of five shillings was also payable when the ticket was purchased, and this would be refunded if the ticket was surrendered not later than the day after it had expired. Season tickets could also be 'deposited', or handed in for one or two months, during which time the ticket could not be used, but a corresponding length of time would be added on to its final validity once the ticket was again required for use.

Major Refurbishment in 1926

The station was closed for most of June 1926 when major refurbishment was carried out by Southern Railway. New signalling equipment accompanied new platforms and track, and the glass roof was cleaned. The same roof was later dismantled, and carefully packed away for preservation. It was stored in a factory before World War II, but ironically, during the Blitz the factory was hit by a German bomb and the roof was completely destroyed.

Station Air-Raid Shelters in World War II

The cellars of the Cannon Street Station Restaurant were used as an air-raid shelter from August 1940. Regular users living close by would bring their own sheets and rugs to sleep on, food to share, and some form of entertainment such as a musical instrument to calm anxious children and to help pass the time, while the sound of bombs exploding above could be heard. The shelter provided enough protection for up to 160 people; sanitation was provided in the form of six chemical toilets and five buckets, with a curtain for privacy.

However, this accommodation was soon found to be inadequate for the 3,022 passengers passing through the station in a ten-minute period during rush hour, and so further basement areas under the station, and the offices that had been the hotel building were also explored as additional areas that could be used. These rooms were extremely complex, built on different levels, making the supply of electricity and water to the cellars quite difficult. The South Eastern Railway was unable to supply the original building plans and so the City of London Engineer was obliged to arrange for a survey to be carried out before the rooms could be fitted out.

By September 1944 three separate shelters were in operation at the station and capacity had increased to 2,980 people, although this number was rarely achieved. The Corporation of London agreed to a request from the Ministry of Works to billet first-aid and repair workers in part of the shelter under Southern House.

Fire Damage in 1941 and 1957

During World War II the station suffered badly from German bombing. On the night of 10 May 1941 both the train shed and the former City Terminus Hotel were hit, and the glazing from the train-shed roof was completely destroyed, as were the top floors of the hotel building. The surviving ironwork from the roof was retained, but a standard ridge-and-furrow roof was built above it, while the top floors of the hotel building were rebuilt in a fairly plain style.

Further disaster struck the operation of Cannon Street Station at 3.30am on Friday 5 April 1957, when an electrical fault started a fire in the signal box. The box itself was a lightly constructed two-storey wooden structure, built in 1926, and located over one of the spans of the bridge over the River Thames. Because of its location on the bridge it was necessarily light in form, and a great deal of wood had been used throughout its construction. One of the cables that carried a 130-volt DC supply from the Cannon Street signal-box battery to Borough Market Junction gave rise to an arc at the point where the cable entered the relay room, and the arc ignited the light weather boarding from which the box was made. The signalman on duty had to be rescued from the box, and despite the actions of those nearby, the resulting fire completely destroyed the signal box, making Cannon Street Station virtually unusable for three days.

The complexity of the signalling system at Cannon Street, and the destruction of the signal box, caused one Southern Region official to state that he could not recall any single incident during the London Blitz that was quite so devastating to the operating system as this fire. Within a month a temporary signal box, much reduced in capacity, was up and running, while a completely new fire-proof box was built near Borough Market on the south bank of the river. This was operational from 15 December 1957 to accommodate a new signal frame, a complex instrument designed to operate fourteen colour-light running signals capable of allowing forty-one possible routes in and out of the station, thirty-nine shunt signals and forty-one point levers. This had then to be connected using many miles of cable to allow the usual 417 trains and 73,000 passengers to return to the station each day.

Post-War Developments and Improvements

Following the damage sustained during the war, and being in need of some general refurbishment, together with its prime location in central London, Cannon Street Station started to become the victim of what might be called unsympathetic development in the 1950s. What remained of the roof was demolished in 1958, and the offices that were once Barry's fine Victorian hotel were knocked down in 1960.

Also in 1960 the Ministry of Aviation considered the installation of a heliport on the top of Cannon Street Station. The advantages of a helicopter pad, next to the River Thames in the centre of London, were obvious. Plans were drawn up, and discussions held with London County Council and the British Transport Commission, but potential noise problems were among several reasons why the project was not taken forward.

From 1962 to 1965 a large office complex was built above the station, not without controversy. The architect chosen to design the office complex was John Poulson, an experienced architect and businessman. He had befriended British Rail surveyor Graham Tunbridge, and had begun to make payments to him and to offer him luxury goods in return for lucrative building contracts, including the one for developing Cannon Street Station. Poulson was tried for corruption in 1974 and received a seven-year sentence. At his trial it became apparent that a short time before winning the Cannon Street building contract, Poulson had paid Tunbridge £200 and given him a suit said to be worth £80. Tunbridge was also convicted, fined £4,000 and given a fifteen-month suspended sentence.

Poulson's building was said to be one of the ugliest in London, being constructed from steel, glass and blue panels. It was bland and uninspiring compared to the ornate Victorian hotel building it replaced. In 2007 the decision was taken to demolish the Poulson building and replace it with another, ultra-modern steel and glass construction comprising offices and shops; however, the resulting construction almost hid the entrance to the station under a dense-looking block, at odds with the station's Victorian riverside towers.

Pressure to make as much money as possible from British Rail property in the 1980s led to the use of the 'air rights' over the Cannon Street Station platforms. 'Air rights' refers to the ownership of the space above any land that you may own. This meant that British Rail could sell the space over the eight platforms, and two office blocks were built using a free-standing, 6,000-ton metal frame, held up by 450 piles bored into the ground. The larger block is known as the Atrium building and is linked to the smaller Riverside building, which protrudes slightly between the riverside towers, and includes a roof garden.

A Fatal Crash in 1991

Cannon Street Station hit the headlines in January 1991 when a Kent commuter train failed to stop and hit the buffers at 9am carrying 800 people. The train was only travelling at 5mph, and despite the driver applying the brakes they did not appear to work on the fifth and sixth coaches, which rose up on to the coaches in front. The train was formed from forty-year-old slam-door coaches, and some passengers had already started to open doors when the accident happened. One person was killed in the crash, and another six critically injured, and around 250 received minor injuries.

The train had been very overcrowded with many unable to find a seat, although the inquiry found that it would have made little difference whether a commuter had been sitting or standing when the incident occurred.

British Rail came in for criticism for continuing to use old rolling stock, but the Secretary of State for Transport, Malcolm Rifkind, countered this by stating in the House of Commons that the first tranche of brand new carriages was being built, and further tranches were due to be ordered later that year. New carriages were the highest priorities within BR's Corporate Plan.

The Plumber's Apprentice

In 2011 HRH the Duke of Gloucester unveiled a seven-foot high bronze sculpture at Cannon Street Station called the 'Plumber's Apprentice'. Created by Martin Jennings, the statue celebrates 400 years since King James I issued a royal charter to the Worshipful Company of Plumbers, the livery hall of which stood on the site of the station from 1690 until it was demolished in 1863 to make way for the station.

Cannon Street Station Today

Today the station is almost invisible from Cannon Street, hidden under and behind office buildings and shops. From the river, however, the two Wren-style towers still mark out the station as an enduring Victorian landmark. The station sees twenty-two million passengers pass through its gates each year, serving as an intermediate station between London Bridge and Charing Cross, connecting the City of London with the south of England and the region south-east of London. ✿

Chapter 10

ST PANCRAS, 1868

ST PANCRAS STATION MAY NOT HAVE been built had it not been for the dubious financial practices of the 'Railway King', George Hudson. Chairman of the Midland Railway from 1844 to 1849, it was he who built up the company from one that dealt mainly with the Leicestershire and Nottinghamshire coalfields to become a major railway company serving both passengers and industry with a

wide and profitable catchment area. He achieved this by gradually taking over four other railway companies: the Sheffield and Rotherham Railway, the Erewash Valley Line, the Mansfield and Pinxton Railway, and the Leicester and Swannington Railway.

Hudson was one of the first railway pioneers to extensively merge railway companies in this way, and although this was a very successful

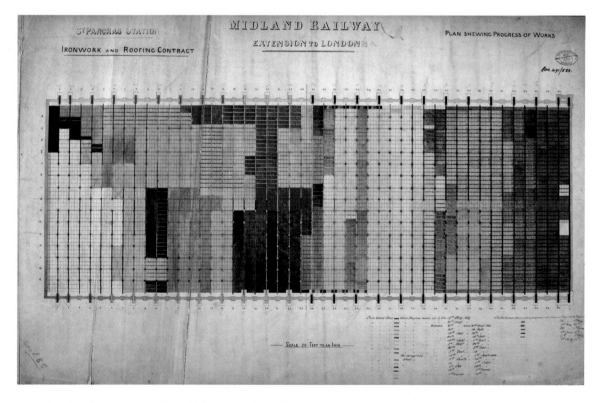

Ironwork and roofing contract drawings of St Pancras Station 1866.   RAIL491/588

An early illustration of St Pancras Station. RAIL1157/1

THE MIDLAND RAILWAY STATION,— S⸱ PANCRAS.

approach to business, he was forced to resign after it became apparent that he was involved in various sharp practices, including paying shareholders out of capital instead of revenue after they had started to receive low dividends. Following an investigation it became clear that he could not continue as Chairman of the company, and he resigned before leaving the country to live in exile in France so as to avoid a prison sentence for debt in Britain.

The new Chairman was John Ellis, a Quaker, an MP and a liberal reformer with a more responsible attitude to the finances of the company than Hudson. He managed to triple the amount of Yorkshire coal, iron and beer from Burton-on-Trent carried by the railway, and therefore put the company on a more solid financial footing. Like many railway company boards, the directors of the Midland Railway wanted to connect

with London, but after the financial difficulties with Hudson they needed time to recover before undertaking any major works. In 1853 the company's railway lines connected with the Great Northern Railway at Hitchin, and in 1858 they agreed running powers over the GNR line down into King's Cross Station, London. They had finally reached their goal, but the arrangement was awkward, and King's Cross Station soon became very overcrowded, with delays a daily occurrence.

A London Terminus for the Midland Railway

Things came to a head in 1862 when the International Exhibition was staged in South Kensington, a world's fair with 28,000 exhibitors from thirty-six countries attracting six million visitors. The Exhibition was built next to the Royal Horticultural Society, where the Natural History Museum now stands, and quite understandably King's Cross Station gave priority to its own GNR trains, leaving Midland trains at a distinct disadvantage – sometimes they even had to deposit passengers at the goods terminal rather than at the passenger station. The Midland board decided they had had enough of playing second fiddle, and that they needed their own London terminus. An Act was passed by Parliament to that effect in June 1863 – and as if to rub the GNR's nose in it, the chosen site was right next to its King's Cross Station, facing on to the 'New Road' as it was then called, now the Euston Road.

The Midland Railway would reach London by extending its line down from Bedford to the new station at St Pancras, a line that would cost the company £9m to build. The site chosen for the new station would prove very challenging in terms of access. The company decided to build four railway lines into the station, which meant a wide swathe of land needed to be cleared through Camden. Parts of Somers Town, and a collection of run-down slums and alleyways known as Agar Town, were completely destroyed.

In retrospect this was no bad thing, since Agar Town was a ramshackle collection of poorly built houses with no street lighting or sewers, and which overlooked the local workhouse and a burial ground on the south side of the Regent's Canal. However, St Luke's church, located on the New Road near King's Cross, had to be knocked down and rebuilt in Oseney Crescent, Kentish Town, and seven other streets were cleared, along with their residents. An estimated 10–20,000 tenants were evicted from their homes without compensation.

The Midland also had the choice of knocking down the gas works of the Imperial Gas Light and Coke Company, or laying their tracks through the graveyard of the St Pancras Old Church. They chose the latter since this would be the cheaper option, although not without controversy. The railway labourers, known as navvies, happily set to work ploughing up bones, coffins and bodies with reckless abandon, so much so that there was something of a public outcry. The author Thomas Hardy, before he was famous, was hired to oversee the work for a short time while training to be an architect, and he later recalled his experiences in a poem called 'The Levelled Churchyard'. Two verses read:

> Where we are huddled none can trace,
> And if our names remain,
> They pave some path or porch or place
> Where we have never lain!
> From restorations of Thy fane,
> From smoothings of Thy sward,
> From zealous Churchmen's pick and plane,
> Deliver us O Lord!

William Barlow's Design for St Pancras Station

Besides the gas works, the River Fleet sewer and the Regent's Canal also needed to be navigated. Overseeing this difficult project was the Midland's consulting engineer William Henry Barlow. He decided to build St Pancras Station on a raised platform, supported by cast-iron columns and girders. This not only solved the problems of crossing the Regent's Canal, and the fact that the land sloped away from it, but it also meant that the ground floor-level undercroft was perfect for storing the beer barrels that would arrive from the breweries of Burton-on-Trent. In fact Barlow later admitted that the design of this level was based on the breweries of Burton-on-Trent, and that the length of a beer barrel became the standard unit by which all the architecture of this floor was measured.

The passenger platforms were therefore at first-floor level, with one track terminus equipped with a hydraulic lift whereby a whole waggon could be let down into the 'cellar' and the beer barrels rolled out on to horse-drawn drays for delivery to local pubs. Barlow also built a separate goods station a short distance away, on the site now occupied by the British Library.

The Construction of St Pancras

The contract for constructing the station and the lines into it was awarded to Waring Brothers. This included the brickwork along the sides of the station and the foundations for the hotel, and these had to be finished by 1 June 1867. The ironwork that formed the roof of the beer vault and the floor of the passenger station above was built on 688 iron piers, each fifteen feet high. This ironwork is in effect a network of ties that hold the roof in shape, and stop the ribs from splaying out and the roof collapsing.

The commitment to quality can be seen by the specifications outlined in the contract, even down to the sourcing of materials. Stone used in the construction had to be either Derbyshire gritstone or Bramley Fall stone from Yorkshire, as used for the Euston arch. Only Derbyshire iron was to be used for the wrought ironwork, and the slate used had to be the best Welsh slate available. Timber was limited to certain types of red pine, or yellow Christiania pine if used for unseen structural support.

The works at the site of the Midland Railway terminal, Euston Road. AN109/1377

The construction of St Pancras. AN109/1377

St Pancras exterior. AN109/1377

Midland Railway extension, St Pancras. AN109/1377

St Pancras interior. AN109/1377

Temporary bridge over Old Street, St Pancras Road. AN109/1377

A separate contract was drawn up for the train-shed roof. Designed by Barlow, the roof comprised a huge 700 feet long, cast-iron and glass single-arched structure, standing 100 feet high at its pinnacle, and 240 feet in width. It was the largest train shed built at that time anywhere in the world, covering 41/2 acres. The contract for construction went to the Butterley Company, a well established and reliable customer of the Midland Railway.

The roof construction was achieved through a massive wooden scaffolding frame, built with the profile of an upturned bowl, and capable of sliding along the platforms as each section of the roof was erected. Huge iron ribs stretching up from brick 'springers' at platform level provided the framework into which the glass panels were inserted. Progress was slow during 1867, and in March 1868 a second wooden scaffold frame was built to help speed things up.

Barlow had originally considered a roof of two or three arched canopies, but these would have been problematic. Firstly, underneath the station two further tracks ran through a curved tunnel linking the station to the Metropolitan Line, giving the Midland Railway access to the City of London, following an agreement signed on 2 September 1867. These were called the 'Widened Lines', and together with the undercroft these structures would have caused problems for any roof pillar foundations; this is one reason why Barlow chose a single overarching roof for the train shed.

A second reason was that the land purchased for the build had been costly, and every square foot was valuable. Barlow was an experienced railwayman, and he knew that creating a vast open station with no pillars, downpipes or obstructions would allow the company to make alterations to the platforms or lines as future planning required.

The station finally opened on 1 October 1868, although it was unfinished. The booking office was not completed until 1869, and there were no waiting rooms or buffer stops. There was no big opening ceremony, although the first new train to leave St Pancras was the 10am express train to Manchester, and it did create a record in that part of its run between Kentish Town and Leicester was the longest non-stop run in the world, at 97½ miles.

A Hotel for the Terminus

While the main station was being built the company directors held a competition in 1866 to design a suitable hotel for the terminus. This was an unusual move, and the directors made their decision without the help of professional architects. The contract was awarded to

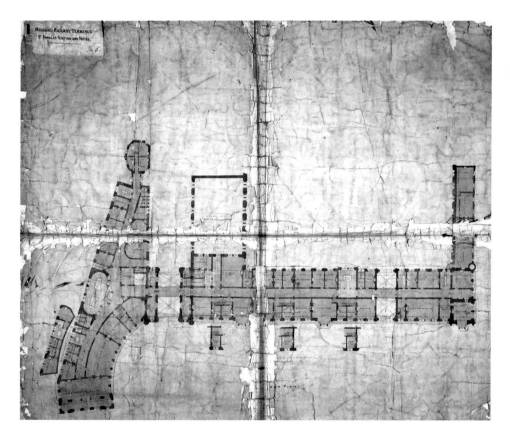

St Pancras' Midland Grand Hotel architectural drawing no. 5, in 1866. RAIL491/1165

The front elevation of St Pancras' Midland Grand Hotel, 1866. RAIL491/580

The Midland Grand Hotel, St Pancras, in the 1870s. RAIL491/833

Sir George Gilbert Scott, who submitted a plan that ignored all the rules of the competition, and was much larger and grander than the directors had requested. But the company had its tail up and went ahead regardless.

The hotel that Scott created was, and still is, one of the most impressive and magnificent 'Gothic revival' buildings in London. It dominates the Euston Road with its great clock tower, numerous elevated spires and pinnacles, rows of decorated chimney pots, huge arches, and the statue of Britannia staring down at the rival King's Cross station. Even the red brick and beige stone from which it is built serve to make the building seem warm and alive compared to the modest, pale King's Cross hotel next door. The hotel appears to incorporate elements of a French château and a Catholic cathedral with its high roofline and rows of arched windows. Christened the Midland Grand Hotel, the lavish decoration continued inside, with a large sweeping staircase welcoming visitors to a Victorian feast of decorated walls, corridors, electric bells and lifts, and gas-lit chandeliers.

The entrance porch to the hotel features two solid columns of polished Shap granite, standing on plinths of the same stone, while the

Midland Railway poster. COPY1/221

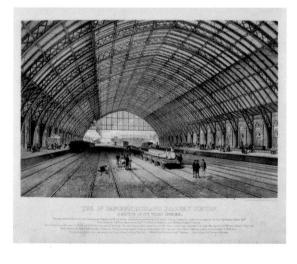

St Pancras, 1869. RAIL491/774

square columns at the corners are made from red stone quarried in Mansfield. The columns support arches of alternating red brick and light-coloured Ketton limestone. The combination of station and hotel architecture serves as one big advertisement, not only for the superiority of the Midland Railway, but also for the quality and availability of craftsmanship and materials from the quarries of the Midlands, Wales and the north of England, all accessible via the Midland Railway network.

The whole building provided 500 rooms, including a ladies' reading room, a smoking room, a billiards room and a dining room over the main entrance. Employees of the hotel were accommodated in the top attics, with separate areas for male and female staff with no communication between them, even having separate staircases. Their accommodation was generous, however, with even the narrowest corridor on the sixth floor being twelve feet wide.

The hotel opened in 1873, and some criticized it for being too ornate. Even Scott himself said in 1870 that 'it is possibly too good for its purpose', while others suggested that Scott had merely resubmitted his earlier plans for the new Foreign Office building in Whitehall, which were rejected in 1856. However, the two plans are very different, and both merely serve to confirm that Scott was an outstanding architect. One anonymous critic writing in the *Quarterly Review* of 1872 criticized the hotel's lavish but unnecessary decoration, saying that 'the eye is constantly troubled and tormented, and the mechanical patterns follow one another with such rapidity and perseverance that the mind becomes irritated where it ought to be gratified'. He added that to be consistent with their theme the Midland directors ought to dress their porters

The Midland Grand Hotel, St Pancras, in the 1870s. RAIL491/833

and attention to detail, so much so that he would personally issue circulars to staff on the most trivial issues. Employees of the Midland Grand Hotel were under strict instruction to make everything as comfortable for the guests as possible. One circular from Towle dated January 1899, and headed 'Special Tables Reserved for Afternoon Tea for Ladies', states that special tables must be set up from 3pm to 6pm for afternoon tea, for ladies only:

> The tables must be nicely prepared with your small cups and saucers, not the ordinary ones used at the counter, and with suitable teapots and a few cakes on one of your stands placed upon the table. You must make the table look as pretty as you can, with a few flowers and a little paper decoration, with perhaps a plant in the centre. A few napkins should be folded up, and the general appearance of the table must be inviting and pretty. You must take care that the tables are specially reserved for ladies and children, and on no account are they to be used for serving gentlemen...

as 'javelin men, their guards as beefeaters, and their station masters [in] the picturesque attire of Garter-king-at-arms'. Another critic took the opposite view, saying that it was 'the most beautiful terminus in London'.

The entrance to the hotel and the roads outside were originally surfaced with small stone 'setts', rather like cobbles. These were hard wearing, but as horses, carts and cabs clattered past the hotel the noise proved too much for the guests. So between 1875 and 1880 the roads were paved with wooden blocks, held in place by rubber inserts, to help make the roads less noisy.

Sir William Towle was in charge of catering and hospitality as head of the Midland Railway Hotels and Refreshment Department. He was an experienced railway caterer from Twyford in Berkshire, and he was driven by good service

Towle's circular no. 34 issued to hotel staff in August 1900 outlined the recipe for a refreshing summer drink: 'In case Cold Bovril & Soda is asked for, the way to make the drink is to put a teaspoonful of cold Bovril into a tumbler, and then add the Soda'. For those unfamiliar with Bovril, it is a meat extract paste used as a savoury spread. Just in case these detailed instructions went astray the recipients were asked to 'Acknowledge receipt'. It is not known whether anyone ever asked for the drink.

The interior of the Midland Grand Hotel. AN109/1377

The interior of the Midland Grand Hotel. AN109/1377

St Pancras Station, 1899, showing the entrances for traffic. COPY1/442

By 1903 it appears that standards had dropped slightly, since Towle issued the following notice on 30 June:

> It has come to my knowledge that in certain of the bars the attendants have been in the habit of pouring dregs from the stout and beer bottles into another bottle kept under the counter for the purpose, and when the same is filled, corking it up, and serving it to the customers.

Apparently the penalty for any future instances of this practice was instant dismissal for the attendant, and for whoever was in charge of the bar.

The Midland Railway Makes Radical Changes

Having been a latecomer to London, and having made its mark by having the most impressive station, the Midland Railway then set about building its customer base by introducing a series of radical changes, bearing out a growing reputation amongst its rivals as a company with an aggressive attitude. In 1872 they opened all their trains to third class passengers, paying just 1d per mile, which no other main line company had yet done. The number of passengers carried subsequently rose by 3.8 million, and their profits increased by £183,000 during 1872. The bad news, however, was that the popularity of second class travel went down, and that many of these carriages were nearly empty. So they needed to find a way to avoid the cost of running empty carriages.

Therefore in 1874 they announced that from the following year second class travel would be abolished, and their first class fares would be reduced to the old second class rates. This left them open to criticism from their rivals, but the Chairman, E. S. Ellis, wrote to the shareholders explaining that their only objective was to increase the profits of the Midland Company by reducing the cost of working the passenger service, and by obtaining a greater number of passengers at lower first class fares.

They also wanted to increase local traffic, rather than take traffic from other companies. They then replaced the bare boards used as seating in third class carriages with upholstered seats, making the budget traveller better off on a Midland train than on any other company's trains. First class passengers were also treated to new levels of luxury with American Pullman cars introduced on a regular service between St Pancras and Bradford in June 1874. The Midland was also the first company to serve hot meals on their trains.

All through the 1870s and 1880s the Midland service at St Pancras prospered – that is, until around the turn of the century when the company began to gain a reputation for lateness. Their timetables were very tight, and with trains covering such long distances, punctuality could not be guaranteed. The popularity of their third class service, and the highly populated major towns through which their trains travelled, such as Sheffield and Nottingham, meant that sheer weight of numbers often slowed progress.

Also the arduous track route down to London, with tight curves and steep gradients, made it almost impossible to keep to the advertised arrival times. Passenger numbers were increasing as the size of the general population rose, and although one solution was to increase the length of the trains, each car carried fewer people due to the introduction of corridor carriages, and the short platforms at St Pancras meant that any train longer than twelve carriages would foul the points at the entrance to the station, thus causing more delays.

St Pancras in World War I

During World War I St Pancras suffered the largest number of casualties suffered by any station, when on the night of 17 February 1918 five German bombs either hit the station or exploded near it, killing twenty-one people (and a dog) and injuring as many others. But despite considerable damage the train service was uninterrupted, although the booking hall and the first class waiting room were wrecked. The 50kg bombs were dropped by the huge wooden Zeppelin-Staaken R.VI four-engine bomber biplane 'R25', one of the largest planes of World War I, piloted by Leutnant Borchers of the Imperial German Air Service.

Declining Fortunes

At the grouping in 1923 the Midland Railway became part of the London Midland Scottish Railway (LMS). Euston station became the new company's principal London terminus, and since the LMS was unable to pay as much attention to St Pancras, its fortunes continued to slide into a sad decline. The Midland Grand Hotel was seen as out-dated, with inadequate bathroom and heating facilities, and in 1935 it was closed and converted into offices for British Railways.

World War II brought more damage and destruction as the station was hit several times during air raids, and in 1943 there were plans to combine St Pancras with Euston and King's Cross to form one large station. After the war, with the nationalization of the railways in 1947, there were several suggestions that the hotel might even be demolished and the station land sold off, particularly during the 1960s, despite a

A view of the damage from a particularly bad air raid on 10 May 1941; the photo was taken from one of the station offices. RAIL421/74

long, slow programme of refurbishment undertaken during the 1950s.

In 1966 it was proposed to amalgamate St Pancras with King's Cross, and turn the train shed into a sports hall. Luckily, in 1967 the hotel and the train shed became Grade 1 listed buildings, which secured their physical survival, even if there was no obvious solution to their purpose. In the 1970s the train-shed roof, which had been damaged in World War II and never completely repaired, was in danger of collapse, forcing British Railways to invest £3m on restoring it.

The Channel Tunnel Rail Link (CTRL)

During the 1980s St Pancras continued to be under-used, and its future looked uncertain. Then in 1994 a new structure seventy-three miles away in Kent provided St Pancras with a real and dedicated purpose. For centuries the idea of a tunnel linking Britain and France had been the idea of ambitious engineers. Finally, on 14 November 1994, the first passenger train ran through the new Channel Tunnel between Folkestone, Kent and Coquelles, near Calais in France. On the French side of the tunnel trains were able to travel at speeds of up to 186mph to and from Paris. But on the English side, speeds were limited to a maximum of 100mph due to the old meandering tracks shared with local traffic, and terminating at Waterloo. In 1996 Parliament passed the Channel Tunnel Rail Link Act, which led to the building of the new railway line: the Channel Tunnel Rail Link (CTRL), also known as High Speed One (HS1).

HS1 was built in two stages, the first stage being started in 1998 between the end of the tunnel and up through Kent as far as Fawkham Junction, near Sevenoaks, in Kent. It opened in 2003, and in tests it allowed trains to reach 208mph, although 186mph was the operational

A view of the damage from a particularly bad air raid on 10 May 1941. RAIL421/74

standard. From there, trains continued at a much slower pace into Waterloo. In 2007 the second section opened, with a twenty-four-mile high-speed track from Ebbsfleet Station, through a tunnel under the Thames near Swanscombe, along the London, Tilbury and Southend line to Dagenham, ending with a twelve-mile tunnel emerging just north of King's Cross, and down into St Pancras Station.

Substantial Renovation for 'St Pancras International'

Not surprisingly the station, now re-branded as 'St Pancras International', underwent substantial renovation during the 2000s, with new platforms built and existing ones lengthened. The lower level undercroft, once used only for beer storage,

was opened up as a passenger concourse, with new shops and cafés built, and a bronze statue of poet and railway station advocate Sir John Betjeman installed, holding his hat and looking up at Barlow's Victorian roof.

During the same period the former Midland Grand Hotel building was refurbished and converted back into a hotel, with additional luxury apartments. It opened to guests on 21 March 2011 with a poignant opening ceremony held on 5 May, exactly 138 years after its original opening.

Therefore, it seems as though an unlikely combination of new technology, the British love of international travel, and our affection for quirky historical Victoriana has saved St Pancras Station for future generations to use and to admire. ✧

Chapter 11

LIVERPOOL STREET, 1874

THE STORY OF LIVERPOOL STREET Station begins in 1835 when a surveyor named Henry Sayer put forward a proposal to build a railway from London to York. After some consideration this plan was thought by Sayer's solicitors to be rather too ambitious, so a shorter line from London to Norwich was suggested. Engineer John Braithwaite drew up the prospectus, and the necessary Act of Parliament was passed on 4 July 1836. Work on the new line began in 1837, and the first section opened on 20 June 1839, running between Mile End in the east of London to the market town of Romford in Essex – and so the Eastern Counties Railway (ECR) was born. A year later the line had extended as far as Brentwood in Essex, and a London terminus had been built for the line in Shoreditch, east London.

However, by this time the ECR was beginning to struggle financially, as landowners objecting to the company wanting slices of their property increased their compensation demands. Building the actual railway line was also becoming more expensive as the terrain away from London was more difficult to traverse. Colchester was reached in 1843, and the line to that point from Shoreditch required the building of sixty-four bridges and viaducts along the fifty-one-mile track. Up until September 1844 the company had used a 5 feet broad-gauge track, but when the ECR took over the Northern & Eastern Railway Company the lines were all converted to the standard gauge of 4 feet 8½ inches.

In 1845 the 'Railway King' George Hudson became Chairman of the ECR, and the finances of the company began to pick up. Hudson took the company forward with some new lines, but concentrated on buying up smaller railway companies, and took steps to link these up so as to give access to the North of England. The ECR took over the Norfolk Railway in May 1848 – but by 1849 Hudson's questionable financial dealings were beginning to catch up with him. He had been paying large dividends to shareholders, while his vice chairman, David Waddington, had been told to amend the traffic accounts to make it look as if these payments had been earned through receipts, which they had not.

On 28 February 1849 the ECR held a very lively Annual General Meeting, and although Hudson failed to attend, within a month he had been forced to resign. Despite this setback the ECR continued to grow and to take over other railway companies, including the East Anglian Railway in 1852 and the East Suffolk Railway in 1859.

A New Station at Liverpool Street

Up to this point the ECR services were irregular, not considered very reliable, and their fares were high compared with similar rail services. Not only that, the Shoreditch station, which had been re-named Bishopsgate in 1845, was too far from the City of London and was too small to cope with passenger numbers, let alone take full advantage of the potential suburban traffic into London. The terminus was stifling the development of the rest of the line, and a new, larger station worthy of this ambitious company was needed. Several locations closer to central London were considered, including Finsbury Circus and Wormwood Street to the south of St Botolph's Church. Then in 1864 parliamentary permission was granted to the company to build a new station at Liverpool Street, through the 'Great Eastern Metropolitan Station & Railways Act'; the following year the ECR changed its name to the 'Great Eastern Railway'.

Before the new London terminus could be built, a large number of low-grade houses and slums needed to be cleared, and the Act of Parliament stated that compensation must be paid to the residents relocated from the area. There were around 10,000 people affected, and they were mainly resettled in the Homerton district of Hackney, with compensation paid at the rate of between thirty and fifty shillings per family. A number of other buildings were also demolished, including the City gas works and the City of London theatre.

As part of the deal the company was required to provide cheap train travel, up to a range of eleven miles from the City of London, both morning and night, for the return fare of 2d. Although this at first seemed like a burdensome requirement, it actually had the effect of generating a solid base of regular commuter traffic from the north-east of London, which proved a valuable investment over the coming years. The north-east region of London was already the capital's most built-up suburb, and the GER's line from Liverpool Street helped to consolidate the area as a home to working-class Londoners, craftsmen and labourers. The new, cheap service resulted in more homes being built in a ribbon of development along the railway route and around its stations, notably at places such as Tottenham, Walthamstow, Edmonton and Leyton.

Ten years after the initial plans were put forward, the new Liverpool Street Station was opened on 2 February 1874, initially to suburban trains only, the line extension and station having cost £2m to build. Bishopsgate, the previous terminus, was closed to passengers in November 1875, and became a goods depot until December 1964 when it was destroyed by fire and abandoned.

Design and Construction

Liverpool Street Station was built on a ten-acre site next to the North London Railway's Broad Street Station. It being a low-level station, builders had to dig down to a great depth through the detritus of centuries of human activity, including old cesspools and sewers. Part of the site was originally where the notorious Bethlehem Hospital – also known as the Bedlam asylum – had stood since the year 1247, where mentally ill patients were held and treated. It is also thought that the site includes an area once used as a mass grave for plague victims from the seventeenth century, and recent excavations have indeed produced a large number of skeletons from this period.

The station was designed by Edward Wilson, a civil and locomotive engineer from Edinburgh, who provided a simple gothic design that was built in stock bricks with Bath stone used for cornices, arches and general dressings. The station building itself was built as a ninety-foot high, L-shaped block facing Liverpool Street; the western wing featured a small clock tower above the booking hall and the waiting and refreshment rooms, and above those were the offices of the GER. In 1923 Lord Claud Hamilton, director of the GER, wrote that the offices 'were built on a faulty and wasteful principle, for many of the rooms are twice the height they need be, and by economy of space, at least another storey could have been added to the whole building'.

In the angle of the 'L' were slopes from street level down to the two sets of platforms. The train-shed roof comprised four large spans of iron and glass, reaching a height of seventy-six feet above ground level. The two large centre spans were each 109 feet in width, while the two outer ones were smaller, at forty-six and forty-four feet wide. The roof was supported by slim, hollow iron columns, which also acted as drainpipes taking water from the roof. Add to this the tall, arched gothic windows located in the side walls, and the overall effect was one of a large church or cathedral.

The station was built with ten platforms, two longer platforms for main line traffic on the eastern side, and eight shorter ones for suburban services on the western side. The platforms were built below street level for two reasons: firstly in order to link up with the Metropolitan Railway, the world's first underground railway, and secondly because it meant that the approach lines would pass below a goods station and under various roads, which was agreed with the City of London Corporation and other bodies.

In retrospect, the decision to build the platforms below ground level was regrettable since every train leaving Liverpool Street had to contend with a sharp 1-in-77 incline out of the station until it reached Bethnal Green. Trains would not normally stall, as such, but they took longer to get going than would otherwise have been the case. The passageways through to the Metropolitan Railway were not used very much, and were removed in 1907, and the long outdoor slopes down from street level to the platforms did not give as good an impression to those entering the station as, say, an imposing flight of steps, or a triumphal arch might have done.

A more practical problem with the station was that the ten lines leaving the station ran out into a four-track bottleneck under the Pindar Street Bridge just outside the station. This meant that only a certain number of trains could leave or enter the station at one time. In 1891 the bottleneck was widened to six lines, and in an attempt to ease congestion, another eight platforms were added to the east side of the station, opening in 1894 and covered by a new, much plainer roof.

This expansion involved demolishing more homes and relocating 700 people to new housing, which the GER were obliged to provide. They also demolished the family mansion of Sir Paul Pindar, a wealthy merchant and diplomat who was knighted in 1620 by King James I. The mansion, which had been built around 1599, was destroyed, but the unique timber frontage, with curved bay windows, was saved and can now be seen on display at the Victoria and Albert Museum.

Local and International Services

With its more convenient situation and low fares the station was heavily used from the start, and by 1902 around 65,000,000 passengers were passing through each year, 90 per cent of passengers travelling from less than fifteen miles away.

The Great Eastern Hotel

No main-line station was complete without its hotel, and the Great Eastern Hotel was added to the site along the Liverpool Street frontage in 1884. It was designed by brothers Charles and Edward Barry, sons of the Charles Barry who designed the Houses of Parliament. They chose a classical French style for the outside of the building, and various styles for the rooms inside. Originally a railway line ran under the hotel, which enabled the easy delivery of food and supplies at night-time. It was also used to deliver sea water from the east coast, for the salt-water baths available to guests staying at the hotel. Anxious to welcome the right sort of people, the hotel had two separate Masonic temples, one decorated in Egyptian style located in the basement, and another in a Greek style on the first floor.

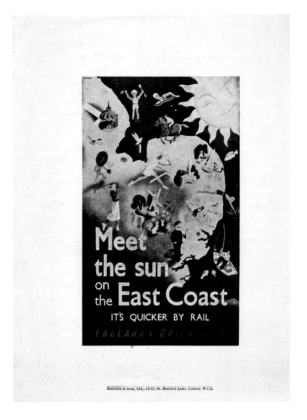

'England's Drier Side' poster, covering rail services from Liverpool Street.   ZLIB15/46/19

These were working-class Londoners travelling to work and home again – but the GER long-haul traffic was also increasing, with new services added through Essex to East Anglia. One of their advertising posters featured a map of East Anglia with people swimming, fishing, playing golf and generally enjoying themselves, with the strapline: 'Meet the Sun on the East Coast – It's Quicker by Rail – England's Drier Side.'

An international element was introduced in 1883, when passengers were able to book a boat-train service from London to Harwich, with a boat taking them from Parkeston Quay to the Hook of Holland, where they could travel on into parts of northern Europe. The service seemed to run very well until the 1980s, when the number of complaints from members of the public started to increase. One problem was that whole trains appeared to contain seats that were 'Reserved' by travel companies, even though most of them were unoccupied, causing confusion and frustration for those travelling individually.

There were also operational problems related to timekeeping, with Liverpool Street trains continually arriving at Parkeston Quay up to twelve minutes late. This meant that Sealink boats would leave the port later than timetabled, and these would then fail to connect with trains in Holland radiating as far as Moscow and Stockholm, giving British Rail a poor reputation across Europe, and giving rise to some lively memos from the Divisional Manager at Liverpool Street who had to deal with complaints 'of international conference proportions'. Parkeston Quay continued to grow, and is now called

Harwich International Port, facing the UK's busiest container port of Felixstowe across the River Stour estuary. The railway station is now known as Harwich International Station.

Liverpool Street Station in World War I

During World War I Liverpool Street Station suffered the largest number of casualties of any British railway station, when twenty German Gotha bomber planes attacked London on 13 June 1917. Three large bombs hit the station, crashing through the train-shed roof and killing 162 people, with another 400 people injured. The station now has a large marble memorial, first unveiled in 1922, listing the names of more than 1,000 GER employees who died in the war, with a later addition, Field Marshal Sir Henry Hughes Wilson, who was assassinated by two IRA men after returning home from having unveiled the same memorial only hours earlier.

The 'Jazz Service'

After World War I, rail passenger numbers were still rising, and many train companies were turning to electrification to improve efficiency. The GER did not have the finances to follow suit, so instead they introduced a new service, doubling the number of trains during rush hour. The public began to call it the 'Jazz Service', and it began on 12 July 1920. This was an intensive commuter service, whereby trains were turned around very quickly, sometimes within four minutes of arrival. On reaching the platform at Liverpool Street, and while passengers were alighting, a new engine would be attached at the platform end of the train, and the original engine

at the buffer stops would be detached and moved to the sidings ready to pull the next train. It was fast and furious, and to help passengers board quickly the first class carriages carried a yellow stripe, while those for second class passengers had a blue stripe. All of this was considered very 'jazzy', hence the name 'Jazz Service'.

Passenger numbers rose to 280,000 per day, with trains leaving the station every one to two minutes during the evening rush hour. Jazz train crews would only be in the station for ten minutes, and then they would be off again on the next journey out, covering the twenty-mile round trip to Enfield three times a day, and making a total of eighty station stops along the way. The GER used N7 tank engines to pull the trains, which were good, powerful steam engines with strong acceleration. Being fitted with Westinghouse air brakes also helped as these worked faster than the old vacuum brakes, and trains were able to run into stations very fast, before braking at the last minute.

The service, which provided trains to Enfield, Walthamstow and Chingford, was highly regarded and reduced the overcrowding of trains without the need for electrification of the line. The only drawback was that the demanding timetable left no room for any further expansion, and following the General Strike in 1926 the Jazz Service was discontinued, never to be replaced.

Electrification

At the grouping in 1923 the GER was subsumed into the London and North Eastern Railway, which then also ran the station; however, it did little in terms of upkeep or innovation apart from overseeing the first electric trains arriving at Liverpool Street in 1949, following the electrification of the line from Shenfield. In fact during the 1930s and 1940s competition from trams and the London Underground gave the steam-powered GER a run for its money, which was always in short supply, and with falling passenger numbers any investment in electrification seemed impractical. However, their long-term resistance to electrification started to give way in the late 1950s, and finally, on 16 November 1960, all services from the station were at last converted from steam power to electricity.

This was the culmination of three years' site work, which included major bridge and station works, new stations built at Harlow Town and Broxbourne, extensive re-signalling work and the erection of overhead line equipment. At Liverpool Street station itself new lighting was fitted, where colour-corrected mercury vapour lighting was mounted at the highest possible level to highlight the classic lines of the building, supplemented by low-level decorative cold cathode lights. As for the rolling stock, new electrically powered carriages were built at York and Doncaster, with fifty-two three-car and nineteen four-car multiple-unit train sets provided for services working out of Liverpool Street.

Cleaning and Renovations in 1938

Due to its position, its design and the nature of its traffic, Liverpool Street gained an unfortunate reputation for dirt and gloom. As the terminus of the most intensive steam-operated suburban train system in the world, it became the victim of vast quantities of smoke, dust and grime. This was compounded by additional pollution from Broad Street Station next door.

During cleaning and renovations undertaken in 1938 some unsuspected ornamentation was discovered, previously hidden by dirt. Two carved brick panels were discovered, the first depicting a ship with two funnels, and the second showing a steam engine coming out of a tunnel. These discoveries were located above the tea-room window in the eastern side of the station, and several other carvings were revealed, illustrating examples of railway work, including a signalman, a fireman, and a porter pushing a barrow. It was thought that the ship represented the GER's shipping service to Holland. A senior official stated at the time: 'They must have been there since the station was built in 1870, but though I have been here for forty-two years I have never seen them before.'

Kindertransport – The Arrival

During the dark days just before World War II, Liverpool Street saw the arrival of up to 10,000 Jewish children, escaping from persecution in Germany, Czechoslovakia, Poland and Austria. They had made the journey from Europe alone, without their parents, via ships arriving at Harwich harbour, before taking the train down to London. To mark these important journeys there is now a bronze statue in the station, unveiled in 2006, featuring five children, carrying their bags, and looking around at their new surroundings. It is called 'Kindertransport – The Arrival' and was created by sculptor Frank Meisler who himself was evacuated from Danzig, Poland, in 1939, travelling with fourteen other Jewish children via Berlin, and through the Netherlands to England. Once in the UK the children were placed in foster homes, hostels and farms around the country. Meisler also created four similar statues, located in Gdansk, Hamburg, Berlin and Rotterdam, marking the route that the children took to escape the hands of the Nazis.

Letter from the British Consulate in Danzig about procedures for the evacuation of child refugees from Danzig to London, April 1939. FO/371/24085/010

W 6549
22 APR 1939

150
BRITISH CONSULATE-GENERAL,
DANZIG.

No. 100.

20th April 1939.

My Lord,

I have the honour to inform Your Lordship that on the morning of April 19th, Dr. Erwin Lichtenstein, Chairman of the Danzig Synagogue Congregation produced to me sixty-nine serially numbered white doublecards, each part of which was about 8" x 5", of identical appearance and content and although the two parts were united they were separable from one another by tearing along a perforated line between them. Each part of these double cards bore a photograph of a child. These photographs were affixed to the cards under an impression of the Royal Arms and the lègend on each part of each card indicated that the child whose name and photograph it bore had been selected for admission to the United Kingdom for education and that the card required no visa. Dr. Lichtenstein also produced a list marked G.AB/EF and dated April 18th 1939 from the British Inter-aid Committee, Bloomsbury House, Bloomsbury Street, London, W.C.1., indicating that these children constituted part of the movement forthe care of children from Germany and that fifty (50) of them were ungaranteed, twelve (12) were guaranteed and seven (7) belonged to the Youth Alijah.

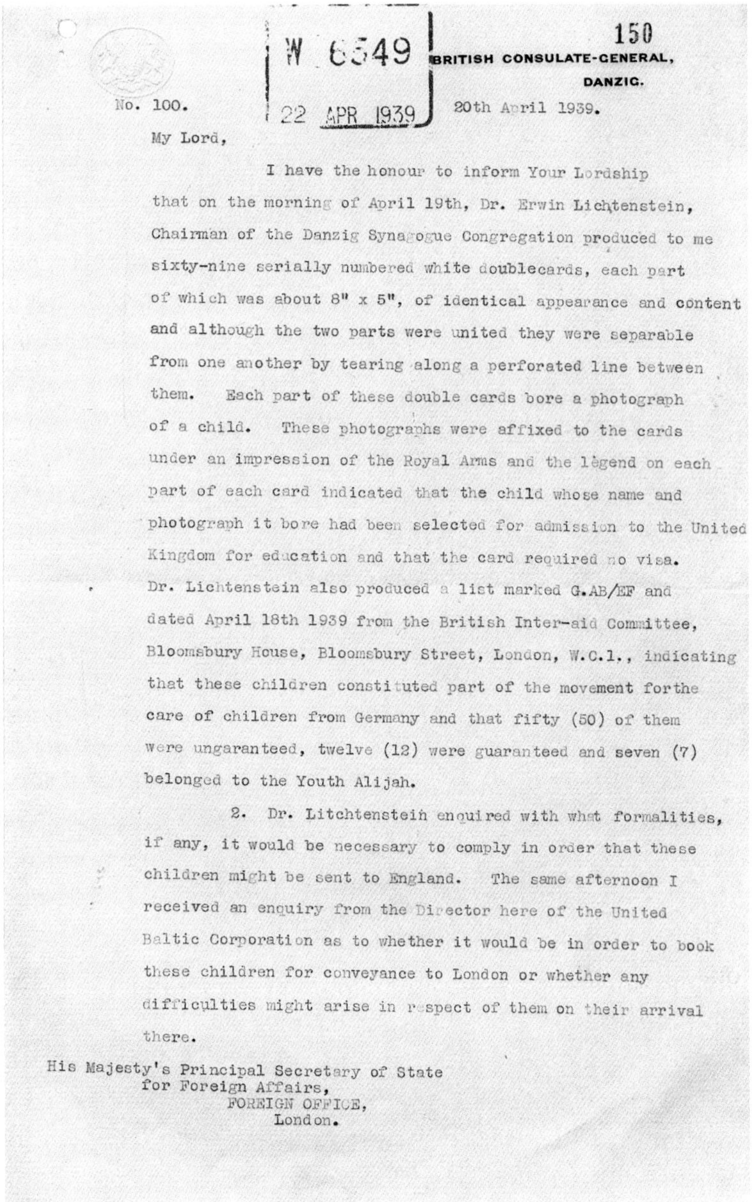

2. Dr. Litchtensteih enquired with what formalities, if any, it would be necessary to comply in order that these children might be sent to England. The same afternoon I received an enquiry from the Director here of the United Baltic Corporation as to whether it would be in order to book these children for conveyance to London or whether any difficulties might arise in respect of them on their arrival there.

His Majesty's Principal Secretary of State
for Foreign Affairs,
FOREIGN OFFICE,
London.

Liverpool Street Station in World War II

On 7 September 1940, the first large-scale attack against London was launched by the German Luftwaffe, involving some 364 bombers, escorted by 515 fighters. Around 2,000 people were killed or injured that night, the first night of what became known as the 'Blitz,' a two-year intensive aerial bombing campaign against London. Early government advice on sheltering from bomb blasts and falling masonry was fairly basic: they suggested using Anderson shelters (corrugated iron sheds half buried in the ground) or

The Kindertransport statue commemorating the children who passed through the station.

order to shelter on the underground platforms. For the rest of the war Liverpool Street Station remained one of the main air-raid shelters in the area for local residents.

However, during 1944 and 1945 the London Passenger Transport Board (LPTB) became aware of a potential disaster awaiting those who took shelter in their tunnels. This may have been as a result of the German move to using the more penetrating V1 flying bombs, and V2 rockets, and the fact that Liverpool Street, being a large building in central London, was an easy target – but the LPTB became very concerned that should a bomb damage a tube tunnel running under the River Thames, then those people sheltering underground in Liverpool Street Station would become trapped, and in all likelihood drown.

In a letter to Treasury Chambers on 2 January 1945, A. J. Edmunds of the Ministry of Home Security stated that the explosion of a rocket falling into the river and breaching a tube tunnel would mean that five tube stations would be flooded to the full height of the tunnel within five minutes, and twenty other stations would suffer similar damage within fifteen minutes. The Treasury therefore gave permission for five flood doors to be installed in the Liverpool Street tunnels, along with klaxon horns, and further discussion ensued as to whether the doors should be automatically closed, since any flood was likely to occur very rapidly.

The plan was that the flood doors would give people enough time to walk through the mile-long tunnel to Bethnal Green Station and make their escape that way. The Corporation of London, however, was concerned that once the doors were closed, no one would be able to leave Liverpool Street Station. With klaxons sounding, bombs falling and the possibility

Morrison shelters (heavy steel table tops with wire mesh sides), or if caught outside the advice was to hide in trench shelters by the roadside, or even to simply sleep out in the countryside. There were some deep underground shelters provided, but they were often overcrowded and insanitary.

During the early days of the Blitz railway and underground station doors were closed, and even protected by barbed wire during air raids. However, the working classes of London's East End could see the logic of using the London Underground stations and tunnels as air-raid shelters, and on 8 September 1940 Londoners forced their way into Liverpool Street Station in of being trapped and drowned underground, it was likely that some elements of the crowd might become alarmed and there could be widespread panic. Indeed Mr Watson, the Shelter Staff Officer, complained that he might have 800 nervous people within locked doors, supervised by only four wardens, adding that 'nowadays wardens are often doddering old boys'.

Some thought that the public should not be told of the dangers of flooding, while others said that rumours had already been circulating, and there ought to be a dress-rehearsal practice evacuation, although this idea was turned down since it would have been unreasonable to ask old and infirm people to spend two hours walking about in the dark. A. J. Edmunds, however, felt that there was no alternative to the overall plan:

> While we do not feel particularly enthusiastic at the prospect of a flock of highly nervous (if not panic-stricken) people having to negotiate a mile of tunnel to Bethnal Green, we do not wish to press our general dislike of the idea to the point of suggesting any modification in the arrangements.

In March 1945 it was agreed that the shelter wardens would be given clear written instructions on what to do in all circumstances – but six months later the war was over, and the great evacuation had never taken place.

Redevelopment: A Modern Station in a Victorian Style

In 1975 British Rail produced a report in which they proposed the complete redevelopment of Liverpool Street Station, and its neighbour Broad Street Station, into one large station with twenty-two platforms. No doubt the plans would have produced an efficient and modern station, but they would also have destroyed the beautiful, quirky Victorian architecture of the building, and as was the case in many other instances of station redevelopment, the poet John Betjeman stepped in. His campaign to save the building led to a public enquiry over the Christmas period in 1976, the outcome of which was a much amended proposal whereby the western train shed of Liverpool Street Station would be preserved, along with the Great Eastern Hotel. The number of platforms would remain at eighteen, but a new combined concourse was built with a new roof extension added at the southern end.

The new additions were sympathetically designed so as to blend into the existing architecture, providing a modern station created in a Victorian style. The land occupied by Broad Street Station was freed up for retail and office development and called the Broadgate Centre, and this would also occupy the air space over the Liverpool Street tracks, the whole development to be known as the Broadgate estate. The eastern train shed did not survive, however, the area being developed into modern offices along Bishopsgate, the work being completed in 1991. Four Victorian-style brick towers were built in 1990, two each at the station entrances on Bishopsgate and Liverpool Street, which help to signpost the entrances and at the same time pay tribute to the heritage of the original station.

King Henry's Mound

One unexpected aspect of the redesign of the station also deserves a mention, an aspect that illustrates the importance that history and tradition still hold in Britain, and which carry more weight than practical functionality. On 19 May 1536 Anne Boleyn, the wife of King Henry VIII, was due to be executed at the Tower of London. Henry needed to know that the execution had taken place, so that he could marry Jane Seymour. So a rocket was to be fired from the Tower of London confirming Anne's death. Tradition has it that the King stood on a mound of earth in Richmond Park, Surrey, in order to gain a clear view of this rocket, and ever since that day this mound has been known as 'King Henry's Mound'.

It is doubtful whether the story is true, since other documents show that Henry was in Wiltshire at the time, but nevertheless the mound does give an uninterrupted view of London to this day. More specifically, it provides a lovely view of St Paul's Cathedral, and the view has been preserved and protected ever since. So when air-space development was being considered for Liverpool Street Station, with a potential skyscraper on the drawing board, the view from King Henry's Mound had to be considered. So much so that the Department of Transport, in drafting their decision letter on the Broadgate Centre in 1978, included the following sentence: 'Additionally, the Secretaries of State are of the opinion that the desirability of safeguarding the attractive view of St Paul's Cathedral from King Henry's Mound in Richmond Park should be borne in mind when detailed designs are produced.'

Liverpool Street Station Today

Today, on entering the station at ground level, you will find yourself on a balcony walkway of coffee shops and retail outlets, overlooking the

Specimen tickets: the top ticket entitles the user to travel from Liverpool Street Station to Gallion's Station.   ZSPC11/345

lower-level station concourse and platforms. Liverpool Street is now a modern, efficient, twenty-first-century railway station, ornamented with actual original Victorian features alongside new elements, which work together, seamlessly balancing the old with the new. The station now looks ahead to playing its part as a major station on the new Elizabeth Line opening in 2018. ✿

Chapter 12

BLACKFRIARS, 1886

The name 'Blackfriars' relates to the area of London where Dominican monks established a monastery in the year 1224, on the east side of Shoe Lane, north of the Thames. It was a large priory stretching about 400 yards from Ludgate Hill down to the River Thames at Puddle Dock. The monks wore long black robes, and were known locally as the Black Friars. In 1538 Henry VIII dissolved the Order, and their priory was pulled down. Forty years later a man named Henry Nailer turned the site into the equivalent of an Elizabethan casino, building several bowling alleys, a pitch on which to play a game called 'Black and White', and a dicing house for gambling.

This was much to the annoyance of local residents, who started a petition against him, writing to Sir Nicholas Bacon, politician and Lord Keeper of the Great Seal, and William Cecil, 1st Baron Burghley statesman, chief adviser to Queen Elizabeth I, Secretary of State and Lord High Treasurer from 1572. The same spot was later used for the Blackfriars Theatre, set up by the actors Richard Burbage and William Shakespeare in 1596. Shakespeare actually bought a house in nearby Ireland Yard, which was the old gatehouse to the original Dominican priory.

Historical Origins of the name 'Blackfriars'

Any history of Blackfriars Station is really about the name 'Blackfriars' rather than the station itself, since there have been three separate stations, owned by two different companies and in slightly different locations but all called Blackfriars, although two have undergone a change of name. There have also been three bridges across the River Thames that have shared the name Blackfriars. It is all rather confusing, and much of it can be attributed to the rivalry between the London Chatham and Dover Railway Company (LCDR) and the South Eastern Railway (SER), which jostled for the best positions for their stations in central London.

The LCDR started out as the East Kent Railway (EKR). It was created mainly as a result of dissatisfaction on the part of local residents and businesses with the existing services provided by the SER, which had built a long and meandering line from London down to Dover via Redhill. This was a tedious route for travellers, and yet many towns in Kent were not served. The first section of the EKR to open was between Chatham and Faversham on 25 January 1858; the line from Strood followed on 13 March, and

Petition by the residents of Blackfriars against the opening of a theatre in the district, 1536. SP12/260

To the right Hon:ble the Lords and others of her Ma:ties most hon:ble privy Councell —/ 176

Humbly shewing and beseeching yor Lordships the Inhabitants of the Precinct of the Blackfryers London, That whereas one Burbage hath lately bought certaine roomes in the same Precinct neere adioyning unto the dwelling houses of the right hon: the Lo: Chamberlaine and the Lo: of Hunsdon, which roomes the said Burbage is now altering and meaneth very shortly to convert and turne the same into a comon Playhouse, wch will grow to be a very great annoyance and trouble, not only to all the noblemen and gentlemen thereabout inhabiting, but allso a generall inconvenience to all the Inhabitants of the same Precinct, both by reason of the great resort and gathering togeather of all manner of vagrant and lewde persons that under collor of resorting to the Playes will come thither and worke all manner of mischeife, and allso to the great pestring and filling up of the same Precinct, yf it should please god to send any visitation of sicknesse as heretofore hath been, for that the same Precinct is allready growne very populous. And besides that the same Playhouse is so neere the Church that the noyse of the Drummes and Trumpetts will greatly disturbe and hinder both the Ministers and Parishioners in tyme of devine service and Sermons. In tender consideration whereof, as allso for that there hath not at any tyme heretofore been used any comon Playhouse within the same Precinct, but that now all Players being banished by the Lo: Mayor from playing within the Cittie by reason of the great inconveniences and ill rule that followeth them, they now thinke to plant themselves in liberties. That therefore it would please yor Lordships to take order that the same roomes may be converted to some other use and that no Playhouse may be used or kept there. And yor Suppliants as most bounden, shall and will dayly pray for yor Lordships in all honor and happines long to live./

Elizabeth Russell
  Dowager
Hunsdon ob 9 Sept 1603
Henry Bowes
Thomas Browne
John Crooke
Will: Meredith
Stephen Egerton
Richard Lee
        Smith
william Paddy
william de Lawne
Francis Hinson
John Edwards
Andrew Lyons
Thomas Nayle
Owen Lochard

John Robinson
Thomas Homes
Ric: Field
Will: Watts
Henry Boice
Edward Ley
John Clarke
Will Bispham
Robert Baheire
Ezechiell Major
Harman Buckholt
John Le mere
John Dollin
Ascanio de Renialmire
John Wharton

227

that to Canterbury on 9 July 1860. Thus began a long-standing rivalry between the EKR and the SER for access to passengers travelling between London and Kent.

In 1859 the EKR changed its name to the London Chatham and Dover Railway (LCDR), in anticipation of the line reaching Dover. Despite always being short of money, the LCDR continued to grow, and in 1861 a western extension was built, taking the line from Strood to Beckenham, where it joined the London Brighton and South Coast Railway (LBSCR), which therefore gave them access to Victoria Station. At last the LCDR had a London terminus, but they had to pay the LBSCR £50,000 per year for the privilege.

At the sixteenth half-yearly meeting of the directors, held on 27 February 1861, Lord Harris, the LCDR Deputy Chairman, gave the following report:

> The present line to the West End [of London] is a very bad one and much longer than is necessary, and in addition we do not have command of the times of the trains that we ought to have. We are obliged to fix our times to suit the trains of the London and Brighton, which are very numerous and a source of inconvenience.

It was clear that the LCDR needed its own access to London.

The LCDR's Independent London Terminus

The Metropolitan Extensions Act of 1860 allowed the LCDR to reach the City of London, by building a 4½-mile railway line from Herne Hill across the Thames to join the Metropolitan Railway at Farringdon Street. The company acquired the land between the river and Southwark Street to the east of Blackfriars Road in 1863, and opened a goods and passenger station called Blackfriars Bridge Station on 1 June 1864, to the south of the river opposite St Paul's Cathedral.

The station was on two levels, the lower one being for goods traffic and the upper one shared between goods and passengers. The upper floor was built on iron columns, which supported iron girders. The building was 420 feet long and sixty feet high, and built from stock bricks with bands of red and pale buff terracotta, with ornamental arches and cornice corbels in the same material. Entrance to the station was via bold arches, and the windows were arranged in pairs, or groups of three, again arched at the top. The front of the building bowed out slightly, and the overall appearance was one of Italianate Gothic, proving an impressive sight for those approaching Blackfriars Bridge from the south.

Blackfriars Railway Bridge

For its first six months Blackfriars Bridge Station was the northern terminus of the LCDR line from Herne Hill, and was a temporary end-of-the-line while the company planned to extend towards the City of London. It was soon connected to the north side of the river by the first Blackfriars Railway Bridge, designed by civil engineer Joseph Cubitt, which also opened in 1864. This took the line north to a new station terminus at Ludgate Hill, opened in 1865. The bridge had large abutments at each end, ornately decorated in bright colours with the company's coat of arms, and those on the south bank have been preserved and restored, and can still be seen today.

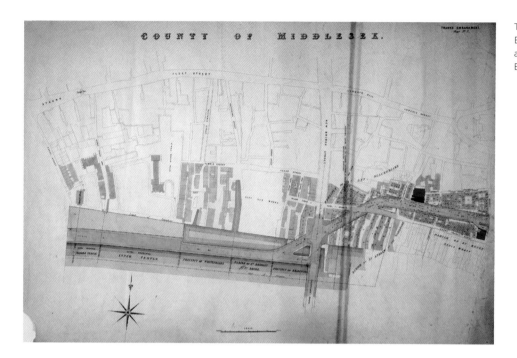

Blackfriars Bridge in 1899. COPY1/439

Blackfriars Road Bridge

Cubitt also designed the nearby road bridge, also called Blackfriars Bridge, making sure that the spans and piers of the two bridges were in perfect alignment with each other. The road bridge was opened on 6 November 1869 by Queen Victoria, who travelled by train in a five carriage procession from Windsor Castle to Paddington, and then to the Surrey side of the bridge where she was presented with an illuminated book containing a short account of Blackfriars Bridge. Having declared it open, the Queen proceeded to the newly finished Holborn Viaduct where a similar ceremony took place, and the viaduct was officially opened to public traffic.

Blackfriars Road Railway Station

In the meantime, the SER had also opened a station named Blackfriars on the line from Charing Cross to London Bridge, situated on the south bank along the Blackfriars Road. It opened in 1864, but only lasted until 1869, when it was replaced by Waterloo East Station. To distinguish this Blackfriars Station from the LCDR station it was retrospectively named Blackfriars Road Railway Station.

St Paul's Station

On 10 May 1886 the LCDR opened their next new station, this time north of the Thames; they called it 'St Paul's Station', and it cost over £750,000. It was fitted with hydraulic buffers of 'enormous resisting power', which were erected at the ends of the three terminal bays. The buffers were a new development in railway safety, and the makers claimed that they would absorb, with the minimum of concussion, the momentum of any train weighing up to 200 tons and approaching at any speed up to six miles an hour. Even if the train were travelling at ten miles an hour, the buffers would arrest its progress with little more than a slight shock, and without causing damage to either the train or the buffers.

St Paul's Station was not a very impressive building compared to other London stations, the company having aspirations but little money with which to express them. As part of the station fabric they included a wall of sandstone bricks into which were carved the names of fifty-four destinations obtainable from the station. These destinations featured localities in the south-east of England, as well as far-flung cities such as Berlin and Baden Baden in Germany, Brindisi in Italy, St Petersburg in Russia, and Marseilles in France. These blocks were preserved and can still be seen as part of the northern end of the current station building today, the lettering having been gilded with 24-carat gold leaf before the blocks were included in the present incarnation of the station.

St Paul's Railway Bridge

Along with the new station a new bridge was built called the St Paul's Railway Bridge, constructed in parallel with the existing railway bridge, slightly downstream to the east. The bridge was built from iron and was designed by John Wolfe-Barry, who also designed Tower Bridge, and Henry Marc Brunel, son of the great railway engineer Isambard Kingdom Brunel. Once this was up and running, Blackfriars Bridge Station on the south bank was closed to passenger traffic, although it continued to be used as a goods station right up until 3 February 1964. It was finally demolished in 1969.

International Business

In common with other railway companies at the time, the LCDR was anxious to promote its international business, as well as its local routes, and in 1885 the company issued a booklet featuring short essays on the destinations served by the LCDR – an early travel brochure.

The booklet began modestly, suggesting that few ways of spending an afternoon are more agreeable than one of 'lounging through the picture gallery at Dulwich' – that is, Dulwich Picture Gallery – which still houses one of the best collections of Old Masters in the world today. The Crystal Palace is the next stop, the great cast-iron and plate-glass masterpiece originally built in Hyde Park for the Great Exhibition of 1851, and relocated in 1852 to Penge Place at the top of Sydenham Hill. Here, the booklet continues, one can take in numerous courts showcasing Medieval, Renaissance, Alhambra, Byzantine, Pompeian, Greek, Egyptian and Italian architectural styles. Further afield one could travel to the seaside locations of Herne Bay, Broadstairs, Margate, Ramsgate or Dover.

But let not the sea stop you: with the company's own cross-channel steamer ship named *The Calais-Douvres*, purchased from the English Channel Steamship Company in 1878, passengers could be in Paris within 9½ hours of leaving London. Other tourist destinations included Brussels, Calais, and the fields of Waterloo in Belgium, where, in the local church, the traveller could see 'marble tablets engraved with the names of the English officers and men who fell on the field'.

LDRC and SER Merger

Whilst its engines were well maintained, the LCDR was often criticized for running dirty and poor quality carriages, and became known for its bad time keeping. In his book *A History of the Southern Railway*, author Colin Maggs writes that the MP for Whitstable informed the House of Commons in 1877 as follows:

> Its trains are formed of unclean cattle trucks propelled at snail-like speeds, with frequent stops of great length, by Machiavellian locomotives of monstrous antiquity held together by pieces of wire, rusty bolts and, occasionally, by lengths of string which clanked, groaned, hissed and oozed a scalding conglomeration of oil, steam and water from every pore.

The tardiness was due in part to the inclines faced by trains on their way up from Kent. As for the shoddy carriages, lack of money was to blame, and in a desperate attempt to keep the company afloat the company had been obtaining loans and selling shares in breach of parliamentary rules. Three men, civil engineer and MP Sir Morton Peto, his brother-in-law Edward Betts and railway engineer Thomas Russell Crampton, had set themselves up as an independent construction company known as Messrs Peto Betts and Company, working for the LCDR. The LCDR had been selling shares and raising money in their name, falsifying the accounts, and keeping the money, paying the three-man construction company in shares.

When the public became aware of this situation, funding dried up and the LCDR was declared insolvent in 1867. Crampton survived the scandal and was able to carry on in business, but Peto and Betts were disgraced and were never able to practise in business again. The Board of the LCDR was completely replaced, and on 1 January 1899 the LCDR was forced into a reluctant merger with its long-term rival, the SER.

The merger made good business sense because the two companies had been competing for customers along the London to Dover route for many years, and even without the LCDR scandal it had become obvious that savings could be made if the two companies were run in tandem. A managing committee was formed to run the two companies as if they were one company; had the companies fully merged, huge tax payments would have been payable, so a complete merger was avoided and they technically remained separate companies.

A new company name was announced on 5 August 1899, the South Eastern and Chatham Railway (SECR), but each original company retained its own identity, with separate shareholders, and all profits being shared in proportion between them. The rolling stock and steamboats of each company were combined and used as one concern, and some new track was laid in order to allow LCDR trains to use SER lines. This situation persisted until the grouping in 1923, when the SECR became part of the Southern Railway (SR).

Business Opportunities for the SECR...

Taking advantage of Blackfriars Station's riverside location, the SECR entered into an agreement with the Thames Steam Tug and Lighterage Company in 1909, to collect and deliver all types of goods at the rate of 2s per ton, to and from the Blackfriars Station wharf. This arrangement covered deliveries all along the river from Chelsea in the west of London, right the way downriver to Tilbury Docks in the east. The arrangement enabled both companies to take advantage of imports and exports at the docks, and to make the most of each other's mode of transport.

There were exceptions to the 2s per ton rate: the most expensive was sulphur, for which the Tug Company was paid 5s per ton, and the cheapest was hearthstone (rough, in sacks), for which only 1s 6d per ton was paid. Interestingly certain other goods were specifically itemized for special rates; this included a product called esparto grass, a fibre produced from two types of North African grass and used in crafts such as basketry. This was transported at the rate of 2s 6d per ton, along with such diverse items as twine, oranges and Canadian hay.

... and Problems

Whilst the River Thames provided many business opportunities for the SECR, it also created problems. The bridge over the Thames needed to be maintained, and this came at a cost in more ways than one.

On 17 June 1907 the iron girders of Blackfriars Bridge were being painted by a team of men working from planks of wood supported by staging irons. The irons were attached to the main girder on the east side of the bridge, and held in place by lugs. At about 8.50am it became necessary to move the staging to another position, and Benjamin Hensman, who was employed as a painter's labourer, together with two other labourers, removed a staging iron and carried it fifty feet along the top of the main girder. His colleagues took the weight of the iron, supporting it by means of a rope, while Hensman attempted to place the top end into position on the girder. He seemed to experience some difficulty in doing so, and then suddenly he slipped and fell sixty feet into the river below.

It was six days before his body was recovered on 23 June, and the accident prompted the SECR to employ a different form of staging from then on, and to provide additional protection to bridge workers by using a safety net.

A Good Safety Record for the SECR

The SECR had a relatively good safety record with comparatively few accidents recorded, partly because of the type of brake used on their trains. This was the Westinghouse air brake system, where air pressure was used to hold the brakes in the 'off' position on each carriage. A loss of air pressure, either deliberately applied by the driver when braking, or through accidental uncoupling, would cause the brakes to be applied. This fail-safe system avoided any possibility of a runaway train.

The SECR also used the 'block' signalling system, whereby a train was only allowed on to a section of track once the signalman had been informed that the previous train had left the section. Thus there was no need for numerous signal boxes, with signalmen overseeing specific sections of track, positioned regularly along the complete length of the line. However, there were always going to be occasions when the unexpected occurred, such as the accident in which Thomas Wellstead was involved on 6 April 1909.

A bill poster by trade, Wellstead worked for the Partington Advertising Company, and had spent the day sticking advertising posters on the outside walls of St Paul's Station. He was using a fifteen-foot ladder, the lower end of which he had placed about two feet from the outer rail of the down main line. He failed to notice the approach of an empty coach train on that line until the engine was very close to him. He quickly attempted to descend from the ladder, but it was too late, and the tank of the engine struck the ladder and he fell to the ground. Luckily his only injuries were a cut to the head and some bruised ribs.

Wellstead, and his foreman George Bennet, both admitted that they had received instructions that no bill poster was to work without a watchman, preferably one employed by the railway company, but evidently this practice had been discontinued at the request of the Partington Advertising Company, possibly on the grounds of cost.

St Paul's Station becomes Blackfriars Station

The SR station continued operating as 'St Paul's Station' until 1 February 1937, when it was renamed 'Blackfriars Station' to avoid confusion with an Underground station which opened on the Central Line, also called St Paul's. At the same time the St Paul's Railway Bridge was renamed Blackfriars Railway Bridge. It is worth noting, therefore, that from 1886 to 1936 there were no passenger stations in London with the name Blackfriars.

The original four-track railway bridge continued to be used right up until 1985, but by then the wooden bridge deck had badly deteriorated, and it was decided that the bridge was too weak to carry modern trains; it was therefore partially dismantled, leaving only the red bridge

Air-raid damage to Blackfriars Bridge resulted in this gap in the tracks – 19 April 1941. MT6/2764

Air-raid damage to Blackfriars Station on 11 January 1941. RAIL648/132

supports in the river, which can still be seen today. Each one is a quadruple-clustered cylindrical pier, topped by foliated capitals, standing on granite and concrete plinths. These have been left in the river because to remove them would have been costly, and the necessary disturbance might have damaged the foundations of the newer bridge beside them.

Modernization for Blackfriars Station

Between 1973 and 1977 Blackfriars Station was completely modernized, with a new entrance hall shared with the London Underground station of the same name, and a raised concourse serving the platforms. Major restructuring again took place at Blackfriars from 2009 to 2012 as part of the Thameslink programme, where the old Brighton main line was rejuvenated to create a commuter service between Bedford and Brighton via central London.

This involved building a new ticket hall at the southern end of the bridge, which opened in 2011, and building through platforms the whole length of the bridge, from one side of the river to the other. This meant that the station could now accommodate trains of twelve carriages, as opposed to the previous eight carriage limit. In order to accommodate these changes the bridge needed to be widened, and the eastern-most run of orange pillars, which used to support the original bridge, were incorporated into the structure of the new, widened bridge. Strengthened and clad in stone, these piers are now hidden inside the modern structure, echoed only by their fellow supports, which can still be seen standing, sentry like, next to the modernized bridge. To the west of the old station new bay or terminal platforms were built for trains terminating at the station.

Actually building a station along a bridge presented its own unique problems. London had not seen buildings on its bridges since 1831 when the old London Bridge and the medieval houses that teetered along it were demolished. In practical terms there was very little storage available on the riverbanks or in the Thames for building materials, so every item had to arrive just in time to be used. Much of it arrived by barge along the river, although the roof trusses were delivered by train. The bridge was widened by nine metres, and over 2,000 workmen were employed at the peak of the construction period.

Approximately 14,000 tons of new materials were used in the new building, the design of which relies heavily on glass and steel. In fact the station has been criticized in some circles for a certain blandness, and a distinct lack of decorative features. However, what it lacks in ornamentation it more than makes up for in technology, being the world's largest solar-powered bridge, fitted and covered with 4,400 photovoltaic solar panels, providing up to 900,000 kilowatts of energy, which is half the daily energy requirement of the station.

Blackfriars Today

The station's redevelopment effectively doubled the station's train handling capacity from twelve trains per hour to twenty-four in each direction. Blackfriars is the only station in London actually to span the River Thames. What could be said to be London's most modern station is now so long that it has two separate postal codes, the southern entrance being in SE1, while the northern end is in EC4V. Blackfriars Station is truly a unique and historic London station. ✧

Chapter 13

MARYLEBONE, 1899

THE BOROUGH AND PARISH OF ST Marylebone have always been associated with affluence and pleasure. The name originates from a church dedicated to St Mary, located next to the Tyburn stream. Another name for a stream was 'bourne', and the church became known as St Mary by the Bourne, later shortened to St Marylebone. However, people have often found it difficult to pronounce. Samuel Pepys called it 'Marrowbone', the eighteenth-century historian Maitland called it 'Marybone', while Prime Minister William Gladstone referred to it as 'Marrilbone'.

In 1659 pleasure gardens and a bowling green were laid out in the grounds of the Rose Tavern on the High Street, and while these were a well used attraction, getting to them from London (still a mile from the city) was hazardous. It was in these gardens that highwayman Dick Turpin saluted Mistress Fountain, saying, 'Be not alarmed, Madam; you can now boast of having been kissed by Turpin!' Doctor Johnson once visited the gardens to see fireworks, and was most disappointed when the rain prevented any kind of display. During the eighteenth and nineteenth centuries a pub located in the Marylebone Road, known as 'The Yorkshire Stingo', was frequented by the author Charles Dickens. Today, situated between the St John's Wood and Mayfair districts of London, and within walking distance of Oxford Street, Marylebone Station is in a prime and prosperous location.

Marylebone Station is the youngest of the great stations in the capital, and was built as the London terminus of the Great Central Railway (GCR), which began life as the Manchester Sheffield and Lincolnshire Railway (MSLR). Their main line stretched from west to east across northern England from Manchester, through Lancashire, Cheshire and South Yorkshire to Sheffield, and on to Nottingham, where any London-bound traffic had to be handed over to other companies. It was always having trouble covering its costs, and many investors referred to it as the 'Money Sunk and Lost Railway'.

Coming south from Manchester and the Midlands, the GCR line was the last main line to be built down to London. Its terminus, Marylebone Station, opened to passenger traffic on 15 March 1899, after the formal opening on 9 March by Mr C. T. Ritchie, President of the Board of Trade. It was the last, and smallest, of the London main-line termini to be built, located in London's largest parish of St Marylebone.

The previous terminus for the company was at Canfield Place near Finchley Road, to the north of London Zoo, and it needed just two more miles of track to reach Marylebone and to be within reasonable distance of London. Sir Edward Watkin, MP and great railway entrepreneur, was the driving force behind the building of the station, after he took over the directorship of the MSLR in 1864.

Watkin was frustrated by a lack of co-operation shown by other railway companies when attempting to run any kind of joint service, and his aim was to run an extension down into London so that his company could provide the full service to the capital. Not only that, he wanted it to be a fast track to London, with a minimal number of stops along the way. His planned route down from Nottingham was therefore through quiet and under-populated countryside. This was to prove a double-edged sword, however, since sparsely populated areas, whilst providing for a speedy service, also meant fewer passengers along the route.

The GCR Extension to London

This new extension down to London changed the whole emphasis of the company, and the new section of the MSLR became known as the Great Central Main Line (GCML). Logically it could no longer be called the Manchester Sheffield and Lincolnshire Railway, and the company changed its name to the Great Central Railway (GCR) in 1897, in anticipation of the new central position it would occupy once the main line to London was up and running.

Watkin was one of the many ambitious Victorian visionaries who helped to change life in Britain, in his case by exercising his love of large-scale railway projects. He eventually became chairman of nine separate railway companies, and one of his ambitions was to develop links from his railways in England to those in France by building a channel tunnel rail link. His Marylebone terminus was really only a link

in the chain, to enable his railways to connect through to the south coast and on to France, via his planned undersea channel tunnel. This dangerous idea was, however, vetoed in 1882 by Parliament, which feared that such a tunnel would leave Britain vulnerable to invasion by the French.

Watkin also attempted to build a British version of the Eiffel Tower at Wembley, as part of his Wembley Park pleasure-garden scheme that was designed to attract people to his railway. He got as far as building up to the first level of the tower before the idea was abandoned. Watkin suffered a stroke in 1894, which meant that he could no longer carry on with his railway work, and it was his successor, Lord Wharncliffe, who oversaw the completion of the GCR London extension to Marylebone.

Although the GCR was much smaller than its rival companies, it was a popular railway and was generally well received by the general public. The new line into London, however, caused some controversy and opposition from the local residents of St John's Wood, a wealthy area of London, and supporters of the Marylebone Cricket Club (MCC) whose Lord's Cricket Ground would be disrupted by the new line. The company wished to acquire sections of the 'Nursery End' of the cricket ground, so called because the land previously belonged to Henderson's Nursery Gardens, which had only just been bought by the MCC three years earlier in 1887.

In December 1890 a public meeting was held in the pavilion at Lords, led by Seager Hunt MP, to marshal support against the proposals, and on 16 December the MSLR sent their man Mr Pollitt to discuss the affair with Mr Perkins, the Secretary of the MCC. Perkins put the case strongly, stating that they had paid £100,000 for the Nursery land,

and he was insistent that nothing would interfere with their plans to enable 'the public to see the finest cricket for 6d each'. Perkins followed this up by a letter to *The Times*, and a rallying call to other cricket clubs in the London area. For a few weeks the deadlock held until Sir Theodore Martin, the solicitor acting for the MSLR, came to an agreement with Mr S. Bircham, the MCC's solicitor, following the cricket club's agreement to purchase extra land from the Clergy Orphan School next door, and an agreement was reached on 20 February 1891. The Railway Bill included a specific clause (Clause 3 of Section 52 of the Extension to London Line Act 1893, to be exact) giving protection to the MCC.

Royal assent was given on 28 March 1893, and it was agreed that a cut-and-cover tunnel would take the line under the east corner of the cricket ground, which would look exactly as it had done before the work began. Work on the tunnel started on 31 August 1896 and was completed by 6 April 1898, when Sir Francis Fox, the GCR's renowned engineer, told Mr Pollitt: 'The work in connection with this cricket ground is now completed, the wall being built and the sodding laid down.' In the meantime the children of the Clergy Orphan Corporation were relocated into the countryside, and the grounds of the orphanage were incorporated into Lord's Cricket Ground.

Construction of the New Railway Line

The new railway line down to Marylebone would be ninety-two miles long starting at Nottingham, running through Buckinghamshire towards Harrow, and then down to London. The route would require eight new viaducts, including the twenty-two arch Brackley Viaduct, and several tunnels, including the Catesby Tunnel, built because the owner of the land under which it travels, Henry Attenborough, insisted that he did not want a railway line on his land. In order to maximize speeds on the line it was built with gentle gradients of no more than 1-in-176 (or 5.7 per cent), and with generous curves of a minimum radius of one mile. New stations on the line were built to the island platform design, with one platform between the tracks, allowing for later expansion of the station and the possibility of new tracks either side if need be. There was only one level crossing on the entire route.

Design and Construction of Marylebone Station

The London terminus was built just north of Marylebone Road, on Melcombe Place in central London, between Harewood Avenue and Boston Place. It occupies the site of what was once known as Harewood Square, whose residents included Sir George Hayter, sergeant painter to the Queen, and John Graham Lough, self-taught sculptor. As the GCR was short on funds, it could not afford to employ an architect, so the station was designed by the GCR's civil engineer Henry William Braddock. It was fashioned to go well with the local housing, incorporating Dutch gables and a homely, Tudor-style red brick, combined with terracotta dressings. The poet John Betjeman described it as resembling a 'public library from Nottingham, which has unexpectedly found itself in London'.

It was built with only four platforms, half the number that were originally planned, but costs prevented the other four from being built. The station survived with only three walls for most of its life, as the fourth northern wall was expected to be added after the other platforms were built at a later date. Consequently the spacious concourse seems a little too large for the size of the station, and indeed for the light passenger numbers using it.

Passenger usage was always low, due to the fact that Marylebone was the last main line station to arrive in London, and most travellers used the much busier and well established London termini. It is reported that the first three passenger trains out of Marylebone station carried only fifty-five passengers between them, and in the early years of its life it was not unusual for the number of porters in attendance on an arriving train to exceed the number of passengers. However, Marylebone Station's adjoining freight depot was well used, which meant that on average over half the traffic to the station was goods related. Its twenty-eight acre goods depot was the largest in London.

The Service from Marylebone Station

The initial service in 1899 comprised only eight trains each way per day, and only two of these served intermediate stations. No GCR trains served stations closer to London than Calvert Station, which was sixty-five miles away from Marylebone. Interestingly, although the station was named Calvert, no such place existed at the time. The name was the original surname of the local landowner, Sir Harry Verney, who had been born a Calvert but changed his name upon succeeding to the Verney baronetcy. This meant that for the GCR there was no suburban commuter traffic at all, and most of their trains were scheduled to attract passenger traffic between London and Leicester or Nottingham,

and places north, almost all the trains being expresses.

Usage quickly increased to fourteen arrivals per day, and by 1958 this had risen to sixty-one, five of which were express trains from Manchester. Over time, as an increasing number of city workers chose to live outside London, the station did evolve into a commuter station, with half the total passengers using the station between 5.30 and 6.30 in the evening.

Quirky Time Keeping

One particular quirk of Marylebone station was that the large station clock over the booking offices was not clearly visible to the guards or drivers of the trains, and so above each ticket collector's gate a small semaphore signal, illuminated by a lamp, was installed. When a train was due to leave the station the ticket collector would lower the signal at his gate, thus advising the train crew that it was time to leave without them having to see the clock.

The Great Central Hotel

Like other London railway termini, Marylebone Station had its associated railway hotel. Sir Edward Watkin wanted to build an impressive hotel that would provide luxury accommodation for his international travellers on their way to France (once he had built his channel tunnel). However, his ambitions were frustrated by the company's lack of money, and the site for the hotel was eventually sold to Sir John Blundell Maple, the businessman and owner of the furniture-making firm Maple & Company.

Maple went ahead and built a magnificent hotel fronting on to the Marylebone Road.

Opened in 1899, the new hotel was called the Great Central Hotel. It was designed by architect Sir Robert William Edis, and built round a large central forecourt. The hotel was linked to the station via a glass and iron awning, which allowed passengers to pass between the two buildings in all weathers. An impressive clock tower watched over the hotel, which was one of the most sumptuous railway hotels in London. It included a number of function rooms suitable for wedding receptions and formal dinners, as well as a ball room said to be one of the biggest in London, capable of accommodating 1,000 people. There was also a Masonic temple in the hotel, so Masons could practise their craft. During World War II the building was used as a hospital.

In 1945 the hotel was converted into offices for the Midland Region of British Rail. In 1986 the building was bought by a Japanese company, and then from 1993 it was refurbished and converted back into a hotel, known as The Regent, London. Two years later it was bought by the Lancaster Landmark Hotel Company; it is currently known as the Landmark London Hotel.

Controversy over the Station Gates

In April 1900 the London County Council (LCC) took legal action against the Great Central Railway over some gates the company had installed outside Marylebone Station. The LCC maintained that the gates were on land owned by the Council, and that the roadway must be left open and unobstructed. They also objected to the shelter that covered the roadway between the entrances of the hotel and booking offices.

The railway company, on the other hand, said that the gates were always open, and that they would only be closed in certain circumstances, such as when royalty were visiting, or to help cope with the movement of troops, for example. The company admitted that the gates had not been included on the original plans, which had been drawn up in haste, but insisted that they were part of a necessary approach to the station, serving to regulate and protect the traffic to and from the entrance. The GCR reasoned that had the gates been included on the original plans, parliament would not have objected to them.

At the hearing on 15 January 1901 Mr Justice Bigham expressed his opinion that the company had acted quite reasonably, that no one had been inconvenienced by the gates, and that the LCC had been wasteful in raising the case. However, since the gates had been an unplanned addition, and he agreed that the roadway should always be left open, he felt compelled to decide in the LCC's favour. The gates were therefore removed and can now be seen at the National Tramway Museum, now known as the Crich Tramway Village, Matlock, Derbyshire, where they were erected in the 1970s.

Sam Fay Rescues the GCR from Bankruptcy

In March 1902 (Sir) Sam Fay was appointed General Manager of the Great Central Railway. Fay was a very experienced and professional railwayman, and it seems that he was chosen for his expertise in turning railways around, having already seen great success with the Midland and South Western Junction Railway, which had been going bankrupt prior to him taking charge, and which he successfully brought back into profit. Described by those who knew him as 'short of stature and slight of build', Mr Fay was a man of

SAM FAY, Esq.
General Manager, Great Central Railway.

Sam Fay, the General Manager of the Great Central Railway. ZPER18

singularly distinguished appearance, with pale, well cut features, dark brown eyes, hair and beard, small hands and feet, and erect carriage; it was said of him that he 'carried the air of having just come out of a bandbox' (a hatbox designed to keep headwear pristine). In manner he was quiet and self-contained, with a polished suavity and courtesy that masked, but did not entirely conceal, an iron will.

Since the GCR was also now in a precarious position financially, Fay concentrated on building up suburban services for the company. The cost of the London extension to Marylebone had been over £11 million, whereas the original estimate had been £3 million, and Fay needed to find a way to increase traffic and boost profits. He started by setting up a publicity department for the company under Mr T. W. D. Smith, which started to publish numerous and varied periodicals, including one called *The Homestead*. This

was a quarterly volume, which was basically a travel guide, but which also included particulars of house property, fares, facilities and so on. These magazines not only provided reading matter for passengers, but also encouraged visitors to experience the delights of London, travelling to the capital of course on GCR trains.

Fay also introduced a staff magazine called *The Great Central Railway Journal* in July 1905. He encouraged staff development and loyalty by introducing examinations and opportunities for promotion, and at the same time he also managed to improve services by cutting the journey times between Marylebone and Sheffield.

Another example of the ways in which Fay was open to new methods, and to increase awareness of the GCR while raising money, was the travelling advertising sign. On 31 December 1906 Fay signed an agreement with the advertising contractors Harry Sanders and William Edgar Woodyer (trading as H. S. Woodyer & Brother) to supply a large, motorized, illuminated advertising sign, which would hang from the girders of the Marylebone Station roof, and would travel across the station between the parcels office and the public lavatory on the other side of the station.

The sign would take the form of a rectangular box, twenty-five feet long, seven feet high and five feet across, with nine individual panels capable of taking separate advertisements or signs, one of which would be reserved for the GCR, provided free of charge. The sign would travel on rails fixed to the roof, and its lettering would change colour as it travelled. Woodyer & Brother would pay all costs associated with the sign, including installation, electricity and payments to W. H. Smith, with whom advertising privileges on the GCR had already been agreed.

An electrically illuminated travelling advertising mechanism, based on an inverted railway, was surely ahead of its time in 1906, and Fay was open and ready to make the most of it, and any other new developments that might come his way. But despite these and other improvements, his efforts were not enough to resolve the fact that the station was always under-used.

The GCR Develops its Tourism Market

By 1911 the Great Central Railway was becoming aware of its tourism market and had started advertising day trips from Marylebone station to Shakespeare Country, providing what they called 'The Shortest and Quickest Route'. Available from July through to September, tourists would leave Marylebone at 10.00am and arrive in Stratford-upon-Avon at 12.20am, from where they would be taken by private automobile to Anne Hathaway's Cottage, Warwick Castle, Guy's Cliffe, Kenilworth Castle and Shakespeare's birthplace, before taking either the 4.35pm or 6.43pm train back to Marylebone. Lunch would be provided at the Golden Lion Hotel (which in 1613 would have been known by Shakespeare as 'Ye Peacock Inn'), and the whole trip would take in 196 miles of rail travel through beautiful English countryside, with another thirty-three miles of private car journeys in a packed nine-hour experience. All of this cost a mere 12s 6d, and there was even a dining car for dinner on the return train journey home.

Specially arranged horse-racing trains were also an important and growing feature on the GCR before World War I, again an innovation

Advertisement, Marylebone.   RAIL226/690

RAIL 226/238.

Shakespeare advertisement designed to be shown in Marylebone Station. RAIL226/238

and a similar arrangement was in place for the St Leger and other race meetings at Doncaster. These services, together with special Bank Holiday trains such as the 'Sheffield Special', which provided a non-stop express run of 165 miles in 177 minutes, proved extremely popular with the public.

The GCR's Fortunes Improve

In 1923 the GCR was subsumed into the London and North Eastern Railway (LNER), and with the opening of Wembley Stadium in 1923, and the British Empire Exhibition being held at Wembley Park in 1924, things began to improve for the little station for a number of years. Passenger numbers increased, and a couple of new services to Yorkshire were introduced.

World War II affected Marylebone less than it did other London stations, with comparatively little damage sustained. There were, however, two instances when the station was temporarily isolated – once when a German bomb fell on the approach tunnels, and again when a doodlebug flying bomb severely damaged a signal box. To cope with these problems some temporary platforms were put up at nearby Neasden, so that trains could start and terminate there instead. During the war, passenger numbers increased due to the number of servicemen and women stationed in the countryside between Aylesbury and Leicester, and the consequent booking of weekend trips on forty-eight-hour passes to London and beyond.

Being a relatively quiet station, together with pleasing architecture, Marylebone Station was the ideal location for staging events, or exhibiting new locomotives. The great engineer, Sir Nigel Gresley, visited Marylebone Station in

introduced by Sam Fay. Long trains were sent up from Marylebone for the Grand National at Aintree, comprising saloons and dining cars, the trains running directly to the racecourse station. These services introduced the novelty of a fare which included a good lunch on the way up, and a nice dinner on the way down. Two or three trains were often required for the service,

1937 when he took part in the naming ceremony of the 100th 'Pacific' type locomotive, appropriately christened *Sir Nigel Gresley*. The new engine had been constructed at the Doncaster works, and the naming ceremony took place on Friday 26 November, when Mr William Whitelaw, supported by the directors and officers of the LNER, unveiled the nameplate and presented Sir Nigel with a silver replica of the locomotive.

Gresley designed the first Pacific when he was chief mechanical engineer of the Great Northern Railway in 1922, and it was the first post-war British locomotive to be designed and built by any of the railway companies. The *Flying Scotsman* was the Pacific class locomotive which in 1934 achieved the British rail speed record of 100mph when it travelled from King's Cross to Leeds in 2½ hours. All Pacific engines were much admired, and were noted for their reliability, and their ability to run 30,000 miles without repair.

In a similar vein, Marylebone was also the station chosen to exhibit the newly designed Type 4, 2300hp diesel-electric locomotive, exhibited there on 23 April 1959. This was the first example of 147 of these Class 45s on order for British Rail, although only 127 were actually produced; they were the most powerful mainline diesel-electric locomotives to be built in British Railway workshops, combining diesel engines built by Sulzer Brothers Ltd and electric motors from Crompton Parkinson Ltd. Weighing in at 138 tons each, these engines could reach 90mph, they had a driver's cab at each end, and became known as 'Peaks', although officially they were called Class 45s. They operated from 1960 until the mid-1980s, and were built at the BR Derby and Crewe works.

An Uncertain Future for the Station

By 1948 both long-distance and commuter-traffic numbers were down at Marylebone, and the possibility of closure loomed on the horizon. All express train services stopped in 1960, freight traffic stopped in 1965, and the goods depot was sold off for housing. Most of the old Great Central main line was closed in 1966 under Dr Beeching's cuts, since his report claimed that the line duplicated other lines serving the same purpose. These developments left only two lines into Marylebone: that from Birmingham Snow Hill Station, and that from Aylesbury. It was as though the station was being suffocated.

In 1971 the first closure proposal was made, and this was followed by fifteen years of uncertainty for the station. In 1983 Peter Parker, the Chairman of British Rail, considered closing Marylebone Station in order to save money – indeed to make money, by selling off the assets associated with the station. One unusual option under consideration was to convert the track beds into toll roads for motor vehicles, and various charging models were put forward.

The National Bus Company was interested in converting Marylebone Station into a coach terminal, and converting the first ten miles of railway track out of the station to Northolt into a high-speed roadway reserved for buses only. However, this proposal was not well received, since the engineering costs involved would have been prohibitive, the necessary clearances between vehicles would have been impossible to achieve on the narrow strips of land available, and time savings over existing bus routes (from Victoria, for example) would have been minimal.

There was also the question of increased traffic congestion and pollution around the station, which was located within the Dorset Square Conservation Area, making the station and associated hotel building difficult to alter. After much discussion the scheme was dropped.

With fewer and fewer passengers using the station, a final closure proposal was issued in 1984, based on low traffic patterns for 1982/3, when the UK was suffering from a depressed economy, strikes by railway workers, and rises in rail fares. It looked as if the end was nigh for Marylebone. But then on 30 April 1986 the proposal was withdrawn, and an alternative strategy was adopted by British Rail, based on a programme of cost reduction and positive marketing. A new Marylebone working group was set up within the London and South East Region to oversee improvements to the station and its lines. By now the economy was improving, and there had been an upturn in demand for public transport, with passenger numbers increasing by 10 per cent between Aylesbury and Marylebone.

A new timetable was introduced to maximize passenger usage at peak times, and a new marketing campaign was launched to publicize the station and its services. Further up the line there was even an Open Day at Aylesbury Station, for which the station was repainted. The working group agreed to the sale of various station buildings and the nearby diesel depot site, which raised £3.5m, and the old DMUs ('diesel multiple units' – carriages with built-in engines) were replaced with new Sprinter rolling stock, which had the benefits of reducing journey times and lowering maintenance costs.

Marylebone Station Today

Since the 1980s the station has prospered, perhaps because of the lack of pressure to compete with the other busier stations. It has had the flexibility in timetabling to provide for more luxury excursions, heritage steam-train trips, and the laying on of special trains for specific events. It still runs a regular service to Oxford and Birmingham, with local services to Gerard's Cross, High Wycombe, Banbury, Aylesbury and Amersham. The station was expanded in 2006, with two more platforms providing improved services to Birmingham and Oxford.

Its vintage appearance, together with its relative quietness, has made it popular with film and television producers. It appeared in the Beatles' film *A Hard Day's Night,* where it played Liverpool's Lime Street Station at the start of the film, and then Marylebone Station itself (from a different angle) when the Fab Four reach London. It also appeared in the 1965 spy film *The Ipcress File,* starring Michael Caine, *The Thirty-Nine Steps* released in 1978 starring Robert Powell, the 2014 children's film *Paddington* (bear), and has even been used as a backdrop in the popular TV series *Gavin and Stacey.* In fact, from being condemned and almost sold off in the 1980s as an uneconomic white elephant, the station has survived and prospered to become one of London's most well regarded and popular classic English Victorian railway stations. ✿